The Digital Photography Handbook

DOUG HARMAN • Photography by DAVID JONES

BARNES & NOBLE

NEW YORK

How To Be A Digital Photographer

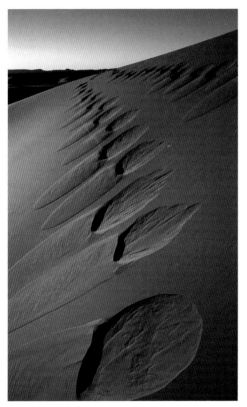

Digital photography offers many advantages – practically, technically, creatively and even economically – over traditional film photography. Over 90% of cameras sold today are digital, but it is the minority of photographers who make the most of the power at their disposal. With a digital camera, you can shoot and store hundreds of photos at practically no cost; instantly review and re-shoot your images; achieve great picture quality; improve your images on computer, correcting badly lit pictures and even repairing old photos; adjust colours and apply special effects; or set up a photo website… the possibilities are exhilarating and nearly limitless.

The Digital Photography Handbook will allow you to make the most of all the advantages your camera has. Assuming no prior knowledge, it will help you quickly to become a true digital photographer – whether you just want to improve your basic technique to get error-free holiday snaps or to learn professional image manipulation techniques for maximum creativity.

This book will take you step-by-step through the four key areas you'll want to master:

1. **Going Digital** – the basics, including choosing a camera and equipment, and getting started

2. **Using Your Digital Camera** – how to take great pictures

3. **The Digital Darkroom** – improving your images on a computer

4. **Output** – getting the best end result, on-line or in print

But although this handbook offers a complete beginner's course in digital photography, you don't have to work through all of its pages to make progress. Each topic makes sense read individually, and you can use the table of contents and comprehensive index to jump to anything you want to know. *Cross-references* in italics direct you to any other useful topics related to a particular subject.

Wherever you start, this book offers a comprehensive reference and is packed with information. But it also draws your attention to the most important things – green and red hint boxes give you instant do's and don'ts to improve your results. Blue highlight boxes focus on the key techniques and knowledge for each topic, speeding the learning process.

Whilst a beginner's guide, *The Digital Photography Handbook* does not avoid any of the seemingly difficult concepts you'll need to know. It demystifies traditionally complex topics such as pixels, depth of field, F-numbers and cloning, explaining them in simple language and using them in practical situations. Any key technical terms you come across can also be found in the glossary for quick reference. In addition, this book will take you, in illustrated steps, through numerous image editing examples, allowing even the novice computer user, working at their own pace, to produce professional results.

Your digital adventure begins here. Enjoy!

Doug Harman

Contents

Going Digital
The basics – getting started

Using Your Digital Camera
Taking great pictures

The Digital Darkroom

Improving your images on a PC

Output

Getting the best end result

Going Digital

In this section, you'll find all you need to get started, including:

 How to choose the right camera for you

 The basics – digital camera features and operation, and camera care

 Camera essentials – what you need to know about memory cards, power and lenses

 Advice on computers, software, printers and other useful equipment

Explanations of megapixels, focal lengths, zoom ratios, resolution, modes and menus, connection speeds, gigabytes, D-SLRs, plug-ins…

Camera Features Explained

Digital cameras are designed to be familiar to anyone who's ever used a film camera. But they have many extra helpful features too...

Most digital cameras have similar basic features. Here we'll introduce you to the typical features of a compact digital camera, and will go on to discuss more specialised functions later in the book. You should check the manual supplied with your camera to see which additional features your camera has.

The Side

PC/AV Socket
Beneath this cover you'll find a socket that allows you to connect your camera to a computer and/or an AV (audio visual) socket that will allow you to display images directly on your TV, depending on the model you own.

DC (Mains Power) Socket
The DC socket allows you to plug the camera into the mains to power it. On some models, a mains adapter will be supplied; if not, you'll need to buy one. Some cameras can recharge their batteries when plugged into the mains.

The Front

Auto Focus (AF) Sensor
The camera uses special sensors to help it to focus automatically. Some types 'sense' changes in contrast (the difference between dark and light areas of scenes) while others use a beam of infra-red (IR) light, particularly in low light. Higher-specification cameras might use a combination of both systems.

Built-In Flash
Most digital cameras have a built-in automatic flash unit that can be used to provide extra light if it's dark, or to reduce shadows on heavily shaded subjects in bright sunlight.

Viewfinder
This enables you to view the scene to be photographed. There are two types: electronic and optical. Using an optical viewfinder means you can turn the large colour screen off, saving battery power. An electronic viewfinder (EVF) uses a little power, but has the benefit of being able to display camera information.

Wrist Strap Lug
You attach the camera's wrist or carrying strap here.

Lens
Most digital cameras come equipped with a zoom lens that enables more or less of a scene to be included by 'zooming' in and out. These changes in focal length are reflected in the viewfinder and on the large display screen on the back of the camera.

The Top

Zoom Lens

When the camera is switched on, the camera's systems are activated. This includes the lens which will extend to its shooting position, ready for action. Zoom lenses are allocated a multiple (or ratio) as a measure of the extent to which they can zoom compared with the lens's focal length. These 'zoom ratios' can be values of up to 10x or more, but a typical digital camera has a 3x zoom lens, which is ideal for most situations (see *Zoom Lenses*).

Shutter Release

The most important button on the camera; it takes the pictures. The shutter release will have two pressures. A half press (and hold) activates the focus system and all the electronics that measure the amount of light available (the light metering system). A little beep, or an 'OK' indicator on the colour screen and/or an illuminated green light next to the viewfinder will indicate that focus has been achieved. Completing the press of the button will fire the shutter and take the photo.

On/Off Button

Your digital camera is electrically powered using batteries and will have a power switch: either sliding the lens barrier or an on/off button.

The Back

Viewfinder (Back View)
This is the part of the camera you use to compose a shot. It also has two small indicators that show the focus and flash status. A green light means the focus is okay, red shows that it is not. If the flash indicator flickers, the flash is charging; when it is steady, it means the flash is ready to fire.

Jog Buttons
This type of 'jog' button is common to digital cameras and allows you to scroll through your images on the large screen. It is also used to navigate through the camera's on-screen menus, the central OK button being used to confirm these selections.

Lens Zoom Control
This switch is pressed at either end to make the lens zoom in or out, making it easy to adjust the view when framing a shot.

Colour Screen (LCD)
The colour screen on a digital camera is great for instantly reviewing your photos to make sure they're okay or for showing them off to others. It can display your camera's settings, menus and picture information. The screen also gives you a live display of your subject, making correct composition easy.

Other Adjustment Buttons
Depending on your camera model, there will be several other buttons on the camera that will be used to control frequently used functions without having to go through on-screen menus. Such functions could include control of the flash, the focus mode or image playback, for example.

Battery and Memory Card Cover
Safely tucked away under a cover, you'll find a place to insert batteries and a socket for inserting the camera's memory card.

Types Of Digital Camera

What kind of camera do you need? Here's a simple guide.

The Basic Digital Camera

A basic digital camera has everything you need to take great photos but in a package that's very simple to use. It will have few – if any – manual photographic controls to play with and most functions will be automatic. These are often called 'point-and-shoot' cameras.

It will include a built-in flash. It will probably have automatic shooting modes you can select such as landscape or portrait setting, and it will have either a fixed focal length lens of around 35mm or it might sport a modest zoom lens.

The resolution is likely to be around three megapixels (3MP) although some basic digital cameras can have lower or higher resolutions (see *How Many Megapixels?* for more about resolution). Note that a camera with a resolution of 2MP or higher will be ideal for 'normal' sized prints (around 6x4 inches).

The Mid-Range Digital Camera

The most obvious differences between basic and mid-range digital cameras, apart from an inevitably higher price tag, are likely to be in the resolution and the lens. A mid-range camera will have a higher resolution of around 4MP or 5MP and almost certainly include a longer, built-in zoom lens. Typically, such lenses have 3x zoom ratios.

However, some mid-range models come equipped with 'super' and 'ultra' zoom lenses. Hence digital cameras can have lenses that provide anywhere from a fixed focal length to zoom ratios of up to 10x, and even higher (see *Zoom Lenses*).

There will also be more manual controls that put you in charge of the photo taking, as well as an enhanced set of automatic controls such as a wider variety of scene modes. You'll notice a marked improvement in sturdiness or 'build quality' on such cameras too.

The High-End Digital Camera

Designed primarily for the advanced snapper, high-end digital cameras (also known as 'Prosumer' or 'Bridge' cameras) are expensive pieces of equipment and feature a multitude of manual controls, backed up by an even more enhanced range of automatic settings.

This camera will have superior internal software that speeds up image capture and processing, making the camera faster and more efficient than mid-range models. The lens may not have a better zoom ratio than cheaper models, but will be crafted from the camera maker's premium optical glass which brings improvements in light-catching ability. Special lens coatings and optical configurations are employed to give improved performance and results.

High-end models tend to have resolutions of 5MP or higher, and can exceed 8MP. They also have versatile flash set-ups enabling the use of accessory flashguns or, for some models, professional studio flash equipment. You'll also get multiple computer connection options providing faster download speeds and connectivity.

The Digital, Single Lens Reflex (D-SLR) Camera

D-SLRs are the very top of the digital camera tree. They are expensive, enthusiast and professional-level high-resolution digital cameras. Some D-SLRs are much more expensive than others, but whatever the price point, the following is a good overview of what you can expect to find should you decide to buy one.

'SLR' is the name given to a camera (digital or film) which lets you view the scene you're photographing through a single 'taking' lens, via a reflex mirror. The reflex mirror directs light from the lens onto the camera's sensor and to the viewfinder (usually) through a special prism called a pentaprism which is mounted inside the camera. This provides the photographer with an exact view of the subject – through the viewfinder – as 'seen' by the lens.

D-SLRs can use interchangeable lenses, not available on a compact digital camera, and this flexibility provides unparalleled shooting versatility. You'll also get all the high-tech gadgetry found on high-end digital cameras, only it will be more specialised or enhanced to give even better performance including resolutions from 6MP up to 22MP.

Add to this a brick-like build quality. Many top-end D-SLRs have toughened bodies for use in poor weather or harsh conditions, where all the buttons and covers are sealed against water and dirt.

How Many Megapixels?

When looking at the sales blurb for digital cameras, you'll see endless mention of megapixels – and this is indeed a critical feature of your camera. So here we'll explain what they are – and how many you'll need.

A digital camera contains a special device, known as a sensor (sometimes referred to as the CCD) to capture light. This replaces the photographic film used in a traditional camera. The sensor is comprised of numerous tiny 'photosites' that collect light, convert it into an electric form and feed it to the camera's on-board computer. Once this digital information is stored in your camera's memory, it can be reassembled on a computer monitor, on your camera's colour screen, or printed to make your photo.

A pixel (from the term 'picture element') is a tiny, discreet location on the sensor that contains the photosite, a micro lens to focus light onto the photosite and other electronics.

The number of megapixels refers to how many millions of pixels the sensor in your camera has. A megapixel is the common term for one million pixels, often abbreviated as '1MP'. A two-million pixel camera will be referred to as 2MP, and so on.

The number of pixels is important because the more a camera has, the more detail it can capture – and the higher its resolution is said to be. Additionally, the more pixels there are, the larger you'll be able to print your pictures. But don't forget, the more megapixels a camera has, the more expensive it will be too.

So how many megapixels should you get when you buy a digital camera? The answer to this depends largely on your budget and what you want to do with your images. You need fewer pixels to post images on the Internet and send them as emails, than to print standard 6x4 inch prints. But you'll need more pixels than that if you want to create enlargements.

For example, you will get perfectly good 6x4 inch prints from a 2MP digital camera and still be able to enlarge the shot to a print size of around 8x10 inches. With 3MP cameras, you'll be able to enlarge your photos up to a full A4 sheet.

If you buy a digital camera with more than 4MP, then you'll be able to print at sizes up to A3 and even larger. So while a less expensive 2MP camera might look like a bargain at first, if you want to create large prints then it's not the camera for you.

Happily, all digital cameras can be set up to use less than their full complement of pixels, so you can tailor shots to their end use, such as the lesser number of pixels needed on an image to be emailed. This is even true with a very high-resolution model. (See the topics *Printing*, *Emailing Photos* and *Creating a Photo Website* for advice on output resolutions.)

Another thing to remember is that the more pixels your camera has, the more memory the shots will use up – per photo – because each image will then be made up from more pixels and so contain more digital information.

High- and Low-Resolution Image Comparison

A single frame of 35mm film contains the equivalent information of around 30MP of data, if it were translated across to a digital camera. But it's not always about the numbers, as the human eye can only perceive a finite amount of detail – around 3MP worth of detail when viewing a print at around arm's length. As has been discussed, the more pixels your camera has on its sensor, the more detail it can capture, allowing you to display or print at a larger size. However, you don't always need all that data.

The following images have each been reproduced to demonstrate how more pixels equal more detail, and lead to differing output image sizes.

High-Resolution 6MP Image

This image has 2000x3000 pixels and has detail and pixels enough for large prints; the colours and detail are all finely reproduced and this image could easily be printed at up to A2 (420mm x 594mm) in size.

Medium-Resolution 1.5MP Image

In this medium-resolution version of the same shot, despite having many fewer pixels (around 1500x1000 pixels), it still has a lot of detail. To the naked eye, it looks almost indistinguishable from the high-resolution 6MP image. This image could only be printed at up to around 5x7inches.

Low-Resolution 0.3MP Image

This low-resolution version of the shot now has only around 640x480 pixels. Normally, this resolution of shot would only be good for use on screen (TV or PC) or for an email for example. If you wanted to print it out, it would only be at a decent quality at around 55x40mm!

Memory & Memory Cards

Every digital camera uses memory of some sort, sometimes called 'digital film'; it provides storage space for your photos as you take them. Here we'll provide advice on how much and what type you need.

The Memory Card Explained

In simple terms, the memory in a digital camera is a small computer chip called 'flash memory' that retains all the data that makes up the photo. Removable memory cards slot into the camera and can be taken out, allowing you to put in a fresh card. Removing a memory card from a camera does not mean you lose the images; they stay safely ensconced on the memory card for downloading or printing later for example.

Those digital cameras with built-in memory capacity rarely have more than enough for a few photos, really just enough to get you started. Many digital cameras come complete with a removable memory card (probably of low capacity) included in the box when you buy them. Either way, you'll need to purchase extra cards almost immediately. The types of cards your camera can use will be indicated in its manual so check before you buy.

Memory Cards at a Glance

There are various types of removable memory cards and they come in a range of capacities, measured in megabytes and gigabytes (MB or GB for short), from around 16MB up to 4GB. The gigabyte is the larger of these two measures and, in fact, 1GB is the equivalent of 1,024 MB. So when comparing memory cards, you should note that a 1GB card has more memory than a 512MB card, for example. The bigger the number of bytes, the more space there is on a card and the more it will cost. Here's a look at the main types.

CompactFlash (CF) Type I and Type II

One of the most popular memory cards, CF has been around for almost as long as digital cameras. They are robust and come in capacities of up to 4GB. IBM MicroDrives are a version of the CF Type II card and are just like miniature computer hard discs that you can place inside your digital camera.

SecureDigital (SD) and MultiMediaCards (MMC)

These two card formats look similar but are not always compatible with every digital camera; cameras that accept SD may not accept MMC for example. They also have different attributes. SD has built-in copyright protection whereas MMC is ideal for multimedia data (hence their

names), such as audio and
image files. MMC is often used
in mobile phones and MP3
players for this reason. A
mini version of SD,
MiniSD, is also now
available. Capacities
for SD can be up to 1GB while
MMC is available at up to around 256MB.

Memory
Stick (MS)

Memory Stick is
Sony's proprietary
memory card format
that is used across many of their products, from
digital cameras to TVs. Memory Stick Pro and
Duo (including 'Magic Gate' cards) are new
versions of this MS format, but the type needed
depends on the digital camera. Capacities range
from 32MB up to 4GB, depending on the format.

SmartMedia (SM)

Available in capacities
between 2MB and
128MB, SM cards are
an older technology,
used by only a few
manufacturers in their
digital cameras. SM
looks likely to be
phased out in coming years, but it should still
be available to buy for a while longer. Bear
this in mind if you're thinking of buying a digital
camera that uses SM cards.

xD Picture
Cards (xD)

A format growing
in popularity, xD is
currently only used
in Fuji and Olympus
digital cameras. It is
extremely small, aiding manufacturers in making
their cameras even smaller. Theoretically, xD can
be made with capacities of up to 4GB but is
currently only available up to 512MB.

What Capacity Cards Should I Buy?

The number of images you can fit onto a
memory card will depend on: the card capacity;
the level of compression applied to the images
in the camera (it varies from manufacturer to
manufacturer); any adjustments you make to the
image resolution (for different quality shots); and
the effective number of pixels the camera has on
its sensor.

To give an example using the 'standard'
memory card supplied with most 3MP digital
cameras – usually only a 16MB card – this will
hold around 20 'standard' quality shots and
between three and five high-quality shots. A
32MB card will hold around 10 high-quality
shots and a 128MB card about 30.

Whilst having one large memory card for your
digital camera might seem attractive and more
cost effective than using a number of smaller
cards, it's better not to have all your 'photo-eggs'
in one basket. Imagine the frustration if you had
a once-in-a-lifetime holiday, shot all your photos
onto one memory card and then lost it! This is a
disaster easily averted if you buy two or three
medium-sized cards. Instead of one 1GB card,
buy one 512MB card, one 256MB card and two
128MB cards for example. It costs a little more
but, in this way, you still have the same total
capacity without the risk of losing all your
photos if something goes wrong.

- Some cameras use more than one
type of memory card. But not every
camera will use every type of card,
so check before you buy. You cannot
use a CF card in a camera that only
uses xD for example.

- Do buy several smaller memory
cards to ensure that all your photos
are not stored on one card. If
something goes wrong, you won't
then lose all the images.

A Buyer's Guide

Choosing a digital camera can be daunting given the huge number of models on the market and their varied features. Here's a quick guide to help you see what's really important when you buy.

The first thing to do is to narrow down the many possible buying criteria to a few key ones. Top of the list will probably be your budget, and then what you need your digital camera for.

What to Spend?

In terms of cost, the most important factors, in no particular order, are simply these:

- As with most things in life, you get what you pay for, so don't scrimp on your investment.

- Remember to budget for a decent size memory card (see *Memory & Memory Cards*).

- Generally, always buy as many pixels as you can afford (see the following descriptions of different resolution cameras for more detailed advice on this).

- Buy a digital camera with a display screen, the larger the better. Without this, you'll miss out on some of the key benefits of using digital cameras: being able to see the shot as it looks before taking it and instantly reviewing it afterwards.

What Do You Need from a Digital Camera?

Before you buy, you need to decide what you want from a digital camera. Once that's done it becomes a much easier decision.

The most common things you might use your digital camera images for are:

- Posting on the Internet
- Sending by email
- Viewing on your PC screen
- Printing out as photographs
- Using for professional work or to make money

Some digital cameras can provide images that are good for all these things; some might not give images that are suitable for any of them. Knowing this is the key to buying the right camera.

Essentially, the number of megapixels (1MP or 3MP for example) that the camera has is the key to the 'tasks' it can perform. It's also worth bearing in mind that the more pixels your camera has, the higher its overall specifications are likely to be and the better its build quality. You'll get bigger pictures and more quality for your money.

The Panasonic DMC FX2, a great, compact mid-range 4MP digital camera, ideal to take anywhere and with enough resolution for good-sized prints.

1MP to 2MP Digital Cameras

For these cameras, the number of pixels that make up the image (the picture size) will be around 1024x768 to 1600x1200. These are very basic digital cameras, fine for posting images on the internet, viewing images on a computer screen or e-mailing. You'll get prints up to a maximum of 10x8 inches in size. It's worth noting when thinking of buying that 1MP and 2MP digital cameras are being phased out and replaced by 3MP and 4MP digital cameras.

3MP to 4MP Digital Cameras

These are the most popular digital cameras and are very widely available. They're also quite inexpensive. A 3MP digital camera has around 2048x1536-pixel resolution and will print photos of around 11x14 inches in size. It should be viewed as ideal for 'general' shooting. However, 4MP cameras provide scope for work that is more detailed and will provide even larger prints, perhaps more suited for professional-style imaging work. Always buy as many pixels as you can afford in this range.

5MP and Above

The current trend in digital cameras is for more and more pixels, which in simple terms offers you lots more detail in your shots. More pixels also means you can make bigger prints, up to and even over A2 in the case of cameras with 8MP and above.

But such cameras are expensive and, even if your budget stretches to it, you don't necessarily need to buy a high-resolution model if you're unlikely to print bigger than, say, A4.

Sony's Cybershot F828 represents the top-end, professional style digital camera, ideal for tough photo tasks and for those who demand a high level of build and specification, with resolution to spare.

MORE PIXELS, MORE DETAIL

In general, it's best to buy a camera with as many pixels as you can afford, as you can always downsize an image if it has more pixels than you need, but you can't upsize an image that doesn't have enough.

For example, if you try to print a 1MP photo at the size you'd normally print a 5MP photo, you see big blocky pixels because you cannot add detail that's not already there. However, you can easily downsize a 5MP image to the usual size of a 1MP image because you have an excess of detail.

Starting To Use Your Camera

Digital cameras are controlled in the same way as a traditional film camera but can also do so much more. Here's a quick guide to the basic operations to help you get started.

Inserting the Batteries

Digital cameras are powered by electricity and so first you'll have to insert the batteries. Over 60% of all digital cameras use AA batteries, but some models use AAA. Cameras that use rechargeable battery packs will come with a charger when you buy them. Charging the battery takes a couple of hours, but they should be fully charged before you begin. (see *Batteries & Power* for more advice on batteries.) Once the batteries are inserted, you can turn the camera on using the on/off switch.

Inserting Memory Cards

Your memory card can only be inserted one way into the special slot on the camera. Once the memory card is inserted, you're ready to start shooting.

A CompactFlash memory card being inserted into a digital camera.

Shooting Controls

The controls that actually allow you to take a photo are the shutter button, and the 'mode' dial. The former is the most important button on the camera as it allows you to focus and fires the shutter, taking the picture. The latter is used to access different shooting functions, to change between playback and picture taking, and to set scene modes (see below).

The shutter button on your digital camera will have two pressures: the first activates the focusing, the second fires the shutter and, as such, it is the most important button on the camera.

Using Scene Modes

Scene modes automatically set the camera up for specific shooting situations and are indicated by small icons on the mode dial or in the on-screen menus, or sometimes both, depending on the camera. Expect to find portrait, landscape, sports and night settings, although some digital cameras have many more. When you select the mode that matches your shot (portrait mode for a portrait and so on), the camera does almost all the work for you.

A typical mode dial will include icons such as those shown here, providing fast activation of the camera's various shooting options simply by turning it to the required mode.

Other Controls

Other buttons provide control over various functions of your digital camera including the menus (see below), activating the flash, turning the screen on and off, and activating the self-timer.

Using Menus

The menus which appear on your camera screen might look daunting at first, but they provide you with a step-by-step series of options for setting the camera up. From changing the date, choosing a resolution or adjusting the brightness of the screen, menus are the heart of your digital camera's settings.

Menus are displayed on the camera's colour screen and provide fast, easy access to the camera settings.

Built-In Flash

The flash lets you add extra, artificial light to a scene that would otherwise be too dark to take a good photo. It can be set automatically or you can manually select it to flash for a particular shot. Additionally, you can use the flash to lift, or fill-in, shadows (see *Creative Flash*) and it also helps prevent unwanted silhouettes if the background is very bright.

The built-in flash provides extra light when shooting indoors or when it's dark.

Movies and Audio Functions

Most digital cameras have movie modes and other functions such as audio clip capture. Movie mode allows you to shoot short 'moving picture' clips of a few minutes, or until the memory card is full. Audio capture can be used to add a short commentary or ambient sounds to your photos.

Connecting to a PC or TV

Digital cameras are supplied with the cables needed to connect them to a PC or TV. Connected to a television, you'll be able to display your photos on a TV screen directly from the camera. Connected to a PC, you can save your images to the PC's hard disc to print them, burn them to a CD or make a slide show as will all be explained later.

Whichever digital camera you own, you'll be able to plug it into a PC using the supplied leads.

Care, Maintenance & Cleaning

If you've invested your hard earned cash in a digital camera, you'll want to look after it. Here are a few simple pointers to help protect your camera and maintain its performance.

A digital camera is a precision piece of electrical equipment and contains many delicate elements, particularly the optics in the lens, the electrical circuitry and the sensor. Each can be damaged quite easily unless you take care.

Camera bags such as this one are an inexpensive and easy way to look after your camera.

Camera Bags

The simplest way to protect your digital camera is to keep it in a proper camera bag. Get a case that's waterproof with decent cushioning and an opening that fastens twice: velcro and a zipper for example. Ensure there's enough room for spare memory cards and a lens cloth.

Protecting Against Dirt and Water

Water and dirt, especially sand, are the digital camera's mortal enemies. If you take your camera to the beach or into the wilds, use a special waterproof 'housing'. This will also keep out sand and dirt. Check with your camera's manufacturer for suitable housings. If you don't have a housing, put the camera back in its bag immediately after use.

- Don't get sand in your digital camera.

- Don't get a digital camera wet. Use a protective housing.

- Don't store a digital camera with the batteries still inside.

Protect your digital camera from water and sand with a waterproof housing such as this one. You'll then be able to take your digital camera underwater too.

- Do use rechargeable batteries - it will save you a fortune.

- Do buy high-mAh-figure rechargeable batteries.

- Do use silica gel if storing a digital camera for any length of time.

Inserting Leads

Many digital cameras come with their own leads made specially for connecting to a PC or TV. So never force a lead into a socket or use the wrong lead. If you damage the socket, the camera will need potentially expensive repairs.

Cleaning

Digital cameras aren't hard to clean - simply wipe them down with a lint-free cloth. Never use solvents or water. If you have a D-SLR and can see dust on the CCD sensor, never, ever clean it yourself. The CCD is very fragile and, despite the fact that you can buy CCD cleaners, if you touch the sensor, it will break. Only get a CCD cleaned by a servicing agent certified for your make of camera.

Storage

If you're not going to use a digital camera for a while, store it in its camera bag with a silica gel pack (it will come with one in its packaging when you buy it). These are small packs containing a gel that absorbs moisture very well. Also remove its batteries or you will risk corroding the contacts inside the camera.

Memory Card Care

Memory cards are NOT affected by airport X-ray machines, but...

- They are affected by magnetic fields. Keep them away from magnets, TV screens and audio speakers.

- Keep cards cool and dry, away from direct sunlight and humidity.

- Keep them away from dust, as this can block the small holes or electrical contacts used to communicate with your digital camera.

- Always keep cards in the protective cases in which you bought them.

You can protect your memory cards too. A case such as this one for xD cards is ideal.

Zoom Lenses

A zoom lens is a key feature on a digital camera as it adds tremendous flexibility to your photography. Here's what you need to know about them.

Most compact digital cameras have optical zoom lenses; that's a lens that can vary its field of view in order to magnify ('zoom in') or broaden ('zoom out') a scene. These are ideal for when you cannot get close to your subject or want to include more of it in the shot, making the camera very versatile.

A 'typical' zoom compact sporting a 3x optical zoom lens.

Focal Lengths

Zoom digital cameras have their focal lengths (the range through which the optics in a lens can move) specified by comparison with the focal length of the familiar ('35mm') film camera. They are indicated on the camera lens in millimetres.

Whilst this may sound confusingly technical, helpfully all you need to know is simplified in the descriptions of digital cameras by using terms such as 'two times' (abbreviated to '2x') or four times ('4x') and so on. The wider the focal range, the greater the 'x' factor (or 'times' factor) becomes and the greater the apparent magnification.

Remember

Buying a digital camera with an optical zoom lens will give you great flexibility in your shot-taking, and the larger the zoom range, the greater the flexibility you will have.

Prosumer digital cameras like this Fuji tend to have longer zoom lenses, in this case 6x.

Here's an example to make all this clear. A digital camera with a zoom lens which has a 35-105mm focal range is said to be a '3x' optical zoom lens, because the highest focal length figure is three times the lowest focal length, i.e. 35 x 3 = 105. A 28-112mm lens would be a '4x', for example, and so on.

The optical zoom range available to digital cameras is growing as lens technology improves and there are now many digital cameras with so-called 'ultra-zoom' ranges with up to 12x optical zooms, offering a focal range of around 35mm to 420mm! The most common digital cameras have 2x or 3x zoom lenses, and while they can't zoom as much as an 'ultra', they are less expensive and just as much fun to use.

These two images show how you can use a zoom lens to improve a shot. By 'zooming out' you can fit everything into a shot, even in confined conditions, as with these men eating at the table. The shot of the balcony, however, was 'zoomed into' to improve detail and the composition with the shadows.

Optical Zoom or Digital Zoom?

Digital cameras, almost without exception and including those that already have an optical zoom lens, have a feature called digital zoom. This can electronically enlarge a portion of the sensor's image to produce a zooming effect.

Optical zoom works by using the lens to magnify the scene and it utilises the entire sensor area for the image, retaining full image quality and resolution.

Digital zoom enlarges a small, central portion of the sensor instead. So it will produce blocky, grainy images and should be avoided if top quality prints are required.

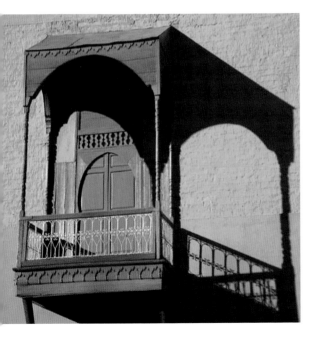

Fixed Lenses

Most cameras come with a zoom lens as standard. But you might want to consider the alternative to these – the fixed lens camera. Here we'll explain which is best for you.

We've seen the flexibility a zoom lens has to offer, but there are a couple of benefits offered by a fixed lens digital camera which are not available to most zoom optics. These are a higher optical quality and a compact size.

Canon's IXUS i5 is a good example of a fixed lens digital camera; it has a high quality build, compact and stylish design, and a bright 39mm lens.

Advantages

Better optical quality results from the lens not being the optical equivalent of a Jack-of-all-trades. A zoom must do a multitude of optical tasks and, in order to achieve them, compromises are made in the lens designs which affect optical quality.

No such compromises are made in a fixed lens. Having one focal length, usually a wide view between 28mm and 35mm, means that the lens is made specifically for that length, making it sharper (for more detail) and

brighter (to let in more light) than the zoom lens equivalent. They often have a wider field of view too.

Compact sizes are possible because the design doesn't cater to the mechanisms needed to zoom the optical train back and forth. Battery power lasts longer too for the same reason.

Disadvantages

Fixed lens digital cameras can seem expensive, largely due to the cost of their optics and the fact that fixed lens digital cameras are often premium models. Another consideration is that there are fewer fixed lens digital cameras on the market. Also, as already discussed, a fixed lens camera doesn't have the convenient flexibility of a zoom. Because of this, most people are willing to live with the compromises involved in a zoom camera.

The Cheaper Option

There are many very cheap non-zoom digital cameras on the market. They tend to use digital zoom to make up for the lack of an optical zoom. We've discussed the problems with digital zoom already, and with very cheap fixed lens digital cameras you actually get worse optics, poor image processing and even poorer results. These are best avoided.

Changing Lenses

You're not always restricted to the lens your camera came with. If you're after more shooting flexibility on a compact, you can use an adapter lens. D-SLRs can use any lens made for them, but there are pitfalls. Here's what you need to know to make the right lens choice.

A digital camera with the ability to use any lens offers the photographer two things: unparalleled versatility and access to superb quality lenses.

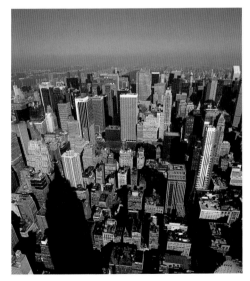

This photo was taken using a wide-angle lens without which you couldn't fit everything into the shot.

Despite the fact that compact digital cameras come with a predetermined focal length range – or just a single focal length for a fixed lens camera – you can still buy specialist lenses and adapters that enable you to stretch your compact's abilities, including wide or telephoto lens adapters. Unlike on D-SLRs, adapter lenses don't replace the original lens – they fit over it.

The interchangeable lenses on D-SLRs are really their raison d'être, allowing you easily to remove a lens and replace it with another of a different focal length. Let's look at how best to adapt or change the lens on each of these types of camera.

Lens Adapters for Compact Digital Cameras

The only way to expand the abilities of a compact's lens when it is an integral part of the camera is to attach something over the front of that lens. Happily, many compact digital cameras come with a screw thread round the front of the lens barrel that provides the means to do just that.

Other types of adapter lenses clip over the front of the camera's entire lens barrel, there are some that strap on, while yet others have special magnetic strips that are used to mount them on the front of cameras. However, the screw-in variety is best as there's less chance of them getting out of alignment and they're less fiddly to use. The other types are, however, cheaper if you're on a tight budget.

Such specialist lens adapters might not offer the same optical quality as a lens made for a D-SLR, but they do provide a way to extend your shooting flexibility quickly and (relatively) cheaply.

Adapter optics are available that provide extra-wide-angle shooting abilities or extend the telephoto end of the lens (the longer focal lengths), providing an increase in optical performance without the drawbacks associated with, say, a digital zoom.

Having said that, optical quality can drop with an attachment, so always buy the lens adapters designed for your camera and, if you can afford it, the ones made by the same camera manufacturer, since they'll be matched to the lens already built into your compact.

Avoiding Adapter Problems

Because adapter lenses are basically a set of new, separate optics that 'bolt' onto the front of an existing lens, there are a few things worth considering before buying.

The adapter lens should be made from high-quality glass of at least as good a quality as that within the camera's lens. If not, expect image degradation.

A wide-angle adapter lens attached to a compact digital camera.

Telephoto and wide-angle converters such as these screw onto the front of your digital camera's lens, providing increased focal range for specific tasks such as zooming closer to your subject or squeezing all of a wide subject into the shot.

This could include 'vignetting', where the corners of shots taken with the adapter will go dark, or an overall softness that's apparent on all shots. It could even make your photos suffer from barrel or 'pin cushion' distortion. The former makes the image bulge in a circular fashion around the middle and the latter pinches the image in at its corners.

LENS FILTERS

Another type of adapter you can attach over an existing lens is a filter. They're not really regarded as a lens, but do provide optical 'special' effects. They include UV filters and polarisers which boost colours, and filters that will change the colour of a scene. They're fun to use but you'll first need to check if you need a special mount to use them on your camera.

- Do buy the adapter lens made specifically for your camera's lens (a 'matched' adapter). This way you'll be able to ensure all the optics are optimised so reducing possible distortion.

- Do buy screw-mounted adapters. They're very secure and offer a light-tight, seamless join with the camera.

Specialist Lenses for D-SLRs

D-SLRs use interchangeable lenses and each make of D-SLR will accept only those lenses specifically made for it; Canon use one type of lens and mount, Nikon another for example. Some independent lens manufacturers such as Sigma or Tamron make lenses that can be used across different D-SLR makes and models, each fitted with the correct mount for the camera to which it will be married.

These lenses are designed to provide a solution to specific shooting tasks from the relatively mundane, such as portraiture where a lens is built to provide the optimal focal length (usually around 135mm) and a flattering blurred background, to extreme close-up (macro) shooting or the ability to take very-wide-angle shots.

In each case, the lens is optimised for its job and, to a greater or lesser degree, will not function as well for other general tasks. So you would ideally need to buy a particular lens for each specific task. They can be very expensive too.

Above: This is Sigma's 12-24mm wide-zoom lens, ideal for squeezing in everyone in a large group at a wedding for example.

Left: Interchangeable lenses are mounted onto a D-SLR camera using a special mount as shown here. Each manufacturer has its own mount type.

- Don't forget that the amount of light reaching the sensor will drop if you are using an adapter lens.

- Don't buy cheap adapters. Image quality will be impaired, distortion will be apparent and you could get horrible pixel fringing too.

The Digital Rangefinder

Also now available is a new type of digital camera, a compact that can use interchangeable lenses, known as the digital rangefinder. The first example of this new breed is Epson's R-D1.

Rangefinder cameras are able to accept a variety of lenses but rather than viewing through the taking lens, as with D-SLRs, you have a 'normal' direct-view optical viewfinder, similar to other digital compacts. The advantages of using interchangeable lenses are the same as they are for a D-SLR. However, rangefinders are not cheap and usually the preserve of the enthusiast and professional snapper.

The Epson R-D1 is the first of a new breed of digital camera, the digital rangefinder, and while it is not as compact as most consumer digital cameras it can use interchangeable lenses.

Which Computer?

If you want to create slide shows of your images or edit and print your own photos at home, a computer is essential. So what should you look for when selecting a PC to use for digital photography?

A personal computer (PC) ideal for digital photography can be thought of as a digital darkroom. What used to be done in an actual 'dark room' full of noxious fumes and poisonous chemicals can now be done in daylight, sipping coffee, listening to music and with relative ease.

Anyone keen on getting hands-on with their pictures, particularly when it comes to playing around with printing, creating enlargements or making slide shows with music and special effects, will need a PC.

What Type of PC?

There are two main types of PC on the market: portable laptop PCs and desktop PCs. Whether you buy a laptop or a desktop is down to the tasks you want do and whether or not you'll want to do them 'on location' and need portability, or work from a fixed location such as your home. Whatever your need, remember that laptops tend to have slower processors, smaller hard discs and (often) smaller screens, but they will probably have built-in wireless connectivity (see *Getting Connected*).

Mac or Windows?

Whether you buy a desktop or laptop, it will use a specific operating system (OS). This is simply a computer program used to make a computer run.

The most common is the Windows operating system. Around 95% of people who own a PC use a Windows PC. They're made by a variety of manufacturers, Dell, IBM and HP are good examples; the latter even produces specific PC systems for digital imaging.

The second main type of operating system is Mac OS used in Apple Macintosh (Mac) computers. Originally designed to be simple enough for children to grasp quickly, Macs do essentially the same job as Windows PCs. Both these types of computer come in laptop and desktop form.

A Mac tends to be more expensive 'off the shelf' but comes loaded with proprietary software – and the right hardware – for imaging. It contains everything you'll need to get started including CD and/or DVD creation, image manipulation, music and slide show software. It's basic but it's there and it gets you started.

A Windows PC has some of this but will not always have the right graphics abilities (it may need upgrading, so be sure to ask before you buy) or the software you might need. However, like Macs, you'll get the basics.

Compatibility

Mac or Windows software can only be used on the type of operating system it's been created for and is not transferable. In other words, once you have a Windows PC you'll have to use Windows software and vice versa. There is emulation software (that makes Windows software run on a Mac for example), but it is not cheap and makes things run very slowly.

Which Features to Look For

You need to ensure that the computer you buy has a large hard disc as this is where all the programs and files are stored. Images rapidly fill up storage space, so buy a PC with the biggest hard disc you can afford but ideally a minimum of around 80 gigabytes (80GB).

Another item to ensure you have in a PC is a 'fast' processor; the processor does all the computing for you. Intel is a well-known manufacturer that makes Pentium processors while another reputable manufacturer AMD makes Celeron processors. Either way it is worth buying a PC with a recognisable brand name such as these. Yes, you'll pay a little more but it will be reliable and fast. Get the fastest available within your budget.

To save space on your desk, buy a computer with an LCD screen. They're very thin and light. Most PCs now have these as standard. A laptop is also good in this respect as it has its screen built into the lid. Larger, old-fashioned style CRT (cathode ray tube) screens are big, heavy and take up loads of room by comparison.

Also ensure you get a PC with a built-in CD/DVD drive, preferably one that can both play and create CDs and DVDs. Check the PC spec carefully for this as there are many variations. Without such features you won't be able to author your own slide shows for example.

Maximise the RAM

There's one simple thing you can do to make your digital imaging experience faster on your PC - maximise the amount of RAM.

Random Access Memory (RAM) is different from 'storage memory' (the hard disc) as your PC uses it to carry out the tasks you give it. All of your commands and the resulting data are processed here, including the data for your photos.

So the more your PC is doing at once, say processing changes to one image while you try to print another, the more quickly the RAM gets used up, and the slower your PC becomes - no matter how 'fast' your PC processor, or how large its hard disc.

But you can avoid this simply by ensuring you have as much RAM installed as you can afford. It's also much cheaper to get extra RAM fitted (if needed of course - check when you buy as your PC may already be 'fully loaded') when you buy a PC. The retailer should be happy to advise and fit it for you too.

Adding RAM is an extra, but not excessive, expense and it will be money well spent.

Computer Accessories

You've got your PC and camera. Now let's see if there are any accessories that will help improve your productivity and make digital work even easier.

Your PC will come with a standard mouse and keyboard enabling you to input instructions and activate some of your system's many features. But there are other devices available that can help make the imaging process even simpler.

Graphics Pads

Using your mouse to carry out image editing tasks is okay, but a graphics pad makes things even easier and more precise. You use a digital pen to 'draw' your changes onto the screen. Working this way is more intuitive and ideal for fine adjustments and intricate image editing work. A mouse is also supplied, as an alternative to the pen, for less precise, general use.

Memory Card Reader

A memory card reader is a small device that usually plugs into the computer's USB port and accepts memory cards. This avoids connecting the camera directly to the PC, therefore speeding up image download to the PC and saving the battery power on your digital camera.

Memory card readers range from those which accept only one memory card to those which allow multiple formats to be used.

External Hard Drives

External hard drives (or 'discs') are an ideal way to extend the storage capacity of your PC. With capacities from 20GB to over 500GB such drives mean you don't need to clutter up your PC's precious hard drive with tons of images and other digital data such as MP3 music files or your digital camera movies. Buy the largest capacity drive you can afford, you'll be amazed how quickly they fill up.

Pen Drives

Pen drives, which have either built-in memory or accept memory cards (as in the Olympus model shown below), are another useful accessory. These are great for quickly swapping data (they save burning a CD for example) and for transferring images from your camera's memory card to your computer, be it a laptop as shown here or a desktop PC.

External CD/DVD Burner

If you have an older system that does not have a built in CD/DVD burner then this item is invaluable. A DVD burner is recommended as it will burn CDs as standard. It enables you to store files, such as slide shows with music and special effects, which you can then transfer to a DVD player and watch on your own TV. Storing files on to CD/DVD also offers a way to back-up huge volumes of image data (see *Backing-Up*) without using up space on your PC's hard disc. Burners are not too expensive either.

Portable CD Burner

A portable CD burner is a useful accessory. They're great for burning images from a memory card when out and about, freeing up space, and can be used as a 'normal' CD burner when back at home or the office. Battery or mains powered, they are a very versatile tool.

Getting Connected

It's all very well having a digital camera, PC and other kit, but now you need to get them to communicate with each other. Here's a guide on how best to get everything connected.

USB Connections

The most common form of connection for a digital camera to a modern PC is a USB (Universal Serial Bus) connection. This has recently been improved with the introduction of USB 2.0 which provides increased data flow speeds. Your keyboard, mouse, printer and scanner probably use USB. All digital cameras have a USB port for connection to a PC, and your camera should come with a USB lead as standard. This makes it very easy just to plug in and connect your PC to your camera, so you can download images for editing and printing. USB also enables 'hot swapping', which simply means you can plug or unplug the cables without needing to restart your computer or the device.

USB 2.0 connectivity makes connection of your camera to your PC or, as shown here, directly to a printer, very easy. It provides fast communication between devices, ideal for printing or transferring images.

Your camera will also probably come with a video lead which will allow you to connect your camera direct to your TV to show pictures on screen.

There are other forms of interface, the name given to connecting various digital devices to a PC, and some systems will have one, two or all of them usually depending on the price of the system.

FireWire

FireWire is technically called IEEE 1394. It is a fast data cable connection common to higher-end digital cameras such as D-SLRs and most modern PC systems. FireWire is faster than 'normal' USB connections but not as fast as USB 2.0 and also hot swappable. You'll also find FireWire on digital camcorders and on some high-end printers and scanners.

Wireless Connections

You'll rapidly see that wires abound with all these interfaces, so if you can afford it, consider wireless networking or WiFi (Wireless Fidelity) connectivity. WiFi devices transmit data in a waveform and can connect together multiple devices, such as a printer, PC or camera, without any cables. Often used

Some digital cameras can connect directly to a printer or PC via a docking station as with this Olympus digital camera, which means no more fiddling with wires each time you want to connect devices.

for notebooks and laptop PCs, WiFi also means you can work anywhere in the home, not just sat at a desk. Any hardware bought that displays the WiFi logo should interconnect seamlessly with any other WiFi enabled device. It can work at distances of up to 350ft, depending on the type of connection.

Each digital camera has a socket into which you can plug its connecting wire, be it USB or FireWire depending on the camera you own.

CONNECTION SPEEDS

It may come as no surprise that the faster the rate at which data is transferred the faster you can work and each of the main connection options has different connection speeds. We don't have to worry about the exact rate they work at, but it's useful to know which is fastest.

- **Bluetooth**: Bluetooth is very slow when compared to cable and to WiFi connections.
- **USB 1.0**: This is pretty much the slowest wired connection and is also being phased out and replaced by USB 2.0, see below.
- **WiFi**: Wifi connections are getting faster all the time but are relatively slow compared with a direct USB 2.0 or FireWire connection. Also, WiFi speed is affected by the number of obstacles in the way (number of walls and the size of the room for example). The latest type (9802.11g) offers the greatest range and speed.
- **FireWire/IEEE 1394**: FireWire is fast and very common and offers connections fast enough for image and video transfer without problems.
- **USB 2.0**: This new USB connectivity allows very fast connectivity and is slightly faster than FireWire.

Bluetooth is another example of wireless networking, and can also be found on many modern mobile camera phones. It is a common wireless interface for up to eight devices over a range of about 30 feet. If you have a Bluetooth enabled printer you could print images directly from a Bluetooth camera without needing a physical wire for example. Not as flexible or fast as WiFi, it still saves on wires.

Which Software?

When you buy a digital camera, it will probably come with a CD-ROM of assorted software, and there are numerous additional imaging programs you can buy. So what software do you really need and what should you use it for?

The Software With Your Camera

The 'proprietary' software that comes with a digital camera is very important as it provides the necessary programs to get your PC and camera talking properly (though depending on the model you buy it may not need – or even have – this software). It will come on a CD-ROM and will be very easy to install by following the instructions in the camera's manual or shown on screen once you insert the disc in your computer's CD drive.

The exact features of the software supplied will depend on your camera model but it usually includes tools to save images onto your PC which then make it easy to sort and search through them. It may also allow basic image editing, although there are additional software packages you can buy that provide more advanced digital imaging tools.

What Image Editing Software Can Do

Why edit your images? Simply, it's an easy way to improve them. For example, you can:

- Resize images for printing or use on a web page
- Improve colour
- Correct exposure problems
- Remove redeye from a portrait
- Crop an image to improve composition
- Make a blurred photo sharp
- Add special effects
- Remove unwanted elements of a scene

How to use image manipulation software to achieve these effects, and many more, is the subject of Section 3 of this book.

What Software to Buy

The following are some of the best software packages you can load onto your computer to enhance your image editing.

Adobe Photoshop CS2
The defacto professional level image editing program is very expensive but comes loaded with everything you might need in order to manipulate photos on your computer. It really is the package to beat.

•Platform: Mac and Windows

Adobe Photoshop Elements 3
Elements 3 is just like a cut-down version of Photoshop CS with only the digital photography 'elements' left in, hence the name.

It is inexpensive but very powerful, and as it is tailored for digital photography it's one of the best to use.

• Platform: Mac and Windows

JASC PaintShop Pro 9
This is similar to Photoshop CS in that it plays host to a full set of professional editing features, but it is a fraction of the price. Crammed full of animated tutorials, this is another stunning package.

• Platform: Windows only

ULEAD Photo Impact XL
Another affordable package replete with excellent features including a web graphics feature and media management. It accepts Plug-ins (small programs that add functionality to the main software package without you having to do any tinkering), thereby boosting its flexibility.
• Platform: Windows only

ArcSoft PhotoStudio 5.5

This package contains powerful editing tools married to an enhanced browser interface with a Photoshop-like feel. Auto editing functions such as redeye removal are included.
This is very affordable and worth trying.

• Platform: Windows only

ULEAD DVD PictureShow
The combination of a basic image editor with CD and DVD burning capabilities makes this a package worth considering as it allows easy archiving to disc and fast slide show creation with music and video. It's easy and inexpensive.
• Platform: Windows and Mac

Adobe Photoshop Album 2
This is a good image organiser that won't bust your budget. It contains excellent features that include a 3D gallery, drag and drop ease of use and powerful cataloguing - essential when your photo collection runs into the thousands.
• Platform: Windows only

Roxio PhotoSuite 5
A package designed for the digital imaging novice, it's a simple-to-use program using easy-to-follow 'wizards' (guides that walk you through each step of a task) and semi-automatic editing functions. It's a superb value package.
• Platform: Windows only

Roxio Toast 6 Titanium
Extremely powerful CD and DVD burner with sophisticated tools for video, slide show, and also music creation. It comes complete with automatic Déjà Vu back-up software.
• Platform: Mac only

Plug-Ins

Want to add even more effects to your pictures, at a reasonable price
or even for free? Read on.

Some image editing software can have extra functionality added using plug-ins. These are small programs that are easily installed on your computer and then work via the software you've added them to. Be it adding specialised black and white effects or adding unusual textures to the look of a shot, plug-ins can help.

Plug-ins can often be downloaded from the web. Some are free and others have a modest cost but either way, if you've got software that can use plug-ins, these are worth considering.

Here are some of the most useful.

Corel Knockout 2

Designed to make hard-to-do cut-outs a breeze, Knockout 2 provides easy-to-use tools for cutting out fine details, such as strands of hair, or transparent areas of a scene (through a glass for example). Also ideal for removing selected areas, such as heads and faces, from one shot and adding them to another, it is a powerful tool to have in your image editing armoury.
• Platform: Mac and Windows

Photowiz Photo Freebies

This is a plug-in that provides a collection of image effects such as sepia, black and white, desaturation (removes colour) and histogram fix all at the click of a mouse. Best of all, it's free to download from www.thepluginsite.com
• Platform: Windows only

Edge and Frame Galaxy

A collection of frames and edges that help give your photos a personal touch and are great fun to play with. Modestly priced, this plug-in can be downloaded from the web at www.thepluginsite.com or is available on CD-ROM.
• Platform: Windows and Mac

Flaming Bear SuperBlade Pro

A great plug-in that allows the creation of new textures and surfaces for your photos, adds bevels, reflections and rough surfaces, and can be stunning when used on text.
• Platform: Windows and Mac

Digital Film Tool Lab

This plug-in simulates the effects of traditional darkroom processing techniques such as 'flashing', over-exposure and low-contrast effects. It's a download from www.digitalfilmtools.com.
• Platform: Windows and Mac

When downloading from the web, only download from sources you think are trustworthy, to avoid the risk of downloading viruses that could damage your computer or files. In fact, it is strongly recommended that you have reputable, up-to-date anti-virus and firewall software installed on your computer if you are going to use the web at all.

Example Effects

The following images are made using some of the demo plug-ins you can obtain as free downloads from the internet.

Each offers a way to expand your creativity but remember, to access some of the better effects you may have to pay for the privilege, though typically such plug-in packages are inexpensive. They are also fun and easy to use, and offer many chances for experimentation.

A background image of a brick wall has been incorporated into this image of a playground swing shadow to make an appealing graphic effect.

Some plug-ins provide a range of frames that can be used to help decorate your images. In this example a brushed (or painted-style) edge has been used with a colour to complement the flower image.

In this shot, a stone texture has been applied to a portrait to add a new dimension to the image.

Plug-ins can provide a series of textured backgrounds to incorporate into your images. Here a metal manhole cover image has been used as a 'reflective' background to this flower image.

Which Printer?

It's really easy to turn your digital images into photographic prints. But you'll need a printer for this and there are hundreds to choose from. Here's a buyer's guide to what you need.

Most digital cameras can print directly from a compatible printer or via a computer, and printing the images yourself provides great flexibility in terms of the size of the print you can make. We deal with the practicalities of printing images in the topic *Printing*, but first here are some tips on making sure you have the right printer.

Inkjet Printers

Inkjet printers are the most common type of printer, designed for general home and office use. They come in many varieties, some being more suitable for printing photographs than others.

Printers don't need to be plugged into a PC or camera, you can print directly from a memory card with memory card compatible printers.

Inkjet printers don't have to be desk-bound as some are extremely portable. Neat in-car cigarette lighter power adapters mean you can print anywhere.

Standard inkjets use a combination of four coloured inks - cyan, magenta, yellow and black - that combine to form the colours we see on a print. But inkjets designed to do high quality photo printing use these four colours of ink plus special photo inks. All such extra inks are designed to improve the colour rendition on the prints and create finer gradations between light and dark areas.

Inkjet printers come in various sizes: A4, A3 and even A2. Some can print on rolls of paper and/or CDs and DVDs so you can customise discs as you go. A4 printers accept 'normal' letter-sized media, and can therefore be used to print both general work and photos. They are very affordable.

Many printers allow you to print on blank CDs or DVDs, roll paper or other specialist media, boosting creativity still further.

You can print directly from some digital cameras with a compatible printer. Plug in the camera and 'drive' the printer using the camera's menus on its colour screen.

A3 printers offer larger print sizes and (sometimes) better colour and print resolution, providing superb print quality, but are expensive. A2 printers tend to be the preserve of the professional and are aimed primarily at studio work; they're very expensive but will produce stunning quality.

Dye Sublimation Printers

Dye sublimation or 'dye sub' printers are designed specifically for printing photos, and offer excellent quality. They come in a range of sizes from 'normal' print sizes (6x4 inches) up to A4. They use a special film coated in cyan, magenta and yellow dyes plus a special fixing layer dye. These are transferred to a special paper which is designed to receive the dyes (or 'sublimated'), using heat.

The downside is that dye sub printers cannot be used for general print jobs such as letters, but if you just want 6x4 inch photo prints a dye sub might be the printer for you.

Printing Without a PC

Most photo printers now have direct printing capability. This allows you to connect the camera to the printer via the supplied connecting lead and produce prints without needing a computer. So if you don't have a PC, you should check you are buying a printer with such capabilities.

Other printers have built-in memory card slots into which you can insert your camera's memory card and print from it directly that way. This type of printer can also act as a card reader, allowing you to download images from your memory cards to a PC, if it's connected. Some digital cameras even have printer-docking stations, allowing for direct printing once they are 'docked'.

- Look for a printer which is a 'true' photo printer (it'll say on the box) and which uses the extra photo inks.
- Inkjet printers with separate ink tanks can be more economical to use.
- Dye sub printers cannot be used for anything other than photos.
- Always buy a 'photo-quality' inkjet printer if photos are the main task your inkjet will be used for.

Which Scanner?

Scanners allow you to bring all your old film photos into the digital domain. Here's a look at what the modern scanner has to offer and which types are available.

Digitising all your old prints, negatives and slides by scanning them onto your PC means you can not only print copies of old photos but you can enhance and restore damaged photos too.

Scanners are easy to operate and allow you to scan images directly to your hard disc, to an email program or even to a printer, at the press of a button. We'll explain how to get the most from your scanner in the topic *Scanning*.

Most scanners come supplied with the software needed to link to your PC and some come with image 'cleaning' software that can be applied to the scan as it is made, removing dirt marks, fingerprints, dust and scratches, which saves a lot of time editing on PC later.

Scanners come in three main types and what you'll need depends on what you want to scan. We'll explain each in turn.

Flatbed Scanners

Flatbed scanners are sometimes called reflective scanners as they capture light reflected off the original document or photo to create an image and are ideal for scanning flat paper and prints. They have an A4 glass platform (called a platen) onto which you place the original photo, document or pages from a book – anything flat really. Some come with a transparency scanning unit (or TPU for short) that additionally allows you to scan slides or negatives. Flatbed scanners are relatively inexpensive and can scan at quite high resolutions, allowing you to put your scans into slide shows for example or make new prints.

This HP flatbed scanner is unusually stylish in that it has a 'photo frame' design and can be used upright saving desk space. It can only scan flat documents and photos, not film.

Film Scanners

Film scanners are dedicated to their task and are designed to scan just film (as opposed to paper prints) of a particular size, 35mm for example. Some, however, have adapters to take other sizes of film such as APS. They are 'transmissive' scanners (in that they capture light transmitted through the negative or slide) and can cope with both black and white or colour negatives and slides. Film scanners use special mounts to hold the film while it's being scanned.

Film scanners also have cleaning software. They are able to use much higher resolutions than flatbed scanners, primarily because the original is typically much smaller. A 35mm

This Nikon film scanner is dedicated to scanning film. It's compact and offers a high resolution capable of producing extremely large scanned image files.

● Do have plenty of RAM and hard disc space in your PC if you intend to buy a scanner as they can create files of many hundreds of megabytes in size.

● Do remember that if you want to scan both prints and negatives, it's necessary to get a flatbed scanner with a TPU.

frame of film for instance is a lot smaller than a normal sized, 6x4 inch paper photograph.

Film scanners are quite expensive, but offer a more professional level of working than flatbed scanners. They provide huge file sizes if needed to make massive prints or for larger scale image use.

'All-In-Ones'

As the name suggests, 'all-in-ones' are combined scanners, printers and photocopiers, sometimes with even a fax built in. These are primarily used where space is at a premium and you don't have room for lots of separate pieces of equipment.

The printer part of an all-in-one is usually of a good standard but the scanner element tends to be of a lower resolution than stand-alone scanners. The latter is also the part that is used to 'copy'. All-in-ones are inexpensive, particularly when compared to buying all three or four machines separately, and make a good general-purpose or home office tool.

How Scanners Work

A scanner can be thought of as a digital camera but one that takes pictures in tiny slices, rather than the whole image at once. The scanner's software rebuilds all the slices back into an image.

A long thin CCD sensor is housed on a motorised arm that moves slowly, in tiny steps, across the original capturing detail as it goes. The resolution (measured in pixels per inch or 'ppi') depends on the number of pixels in the CCD and the number of steps it takes to move across the original document, which the user can adjust depending on the job at hand. The more pixels and steps, the more detail is captured and the higher the resolution and file size.

This is a flatbed scanner from Epson, and has a TPU built into the lid so that you can scan both flat documents and photos, as well as negatives and colour film.

Preventing Camera Shake

It's very easy for camera shake to blur your photos. But there is a range of solutions and support accessories to prevent this.

What Causes Camera Shake?

Camera shake is caused when the shutter speed your digital camera uses is so slow that it is not fast enough to freeze the human body's natural and slight shaking motion – or any other movement for that matter. Such slow shutter speeds come about as a result of using a long focal length which reduces the amount of light reaching the camera's sensor, or just if it is dark.

Preventing Shake by Adjusting Shutter Speed

To prevent camera shake in your photos always use a shutter speed that's the reciprocal of the focal length in use. Therefore, if you use a 100mm focal length, you should use a shutter speed of at least 1/100th second. If you use a 150mm focal length then the shutter speed will need to be at least 1/150th second and so on.

If you cannot control the shutter speeds on your digital camera, then to stop camera shake, you will have to support the camera. Very basic point-and-shoot digital cameras don't always offer control over their shutter speeds so a camera support in the form of a tripod or monopod is essential.

Even when you can control the shutter speed on your digital camera, you still need to keep the camera steady in low light. So when taking a portrait shot or photographing city lights at night, or even a sunset when the sun is very low, a support for the camera will ensure you always achieve a sharp image for your troubles.

Here are some of the best support options.

Tripods

A tripod is a three-legged support with telescopic legs that the camera screws onto via the screw lug on the tripod's mount and the threaded tripod bush on the base of the digital camera. Tripods are quite portable and ideal when using very long focal lengths or in low light.

Tripods come in many sizes, from mini, tabletop models to massive and bulky, professional ones built to keep your camera steady in almost any environment, even in strong winds. Tripods are ideal for shooting landscapes where sharp detail is crucial, long exposures at night or if you want to include yourself in a shot.

Monopods

A monopod – as the name suggests – is similar to a tripod but with only one (mono) telescopic leg designed to help support the camera. The camera mounts on top in the same way as on a tripod, via its tripod bush. It helps to keep the camera steady while still providing a large degree of manoeuverability. Monopods are not as steady as tripods, you have to hold them and they require a little practice to use properly. They do however offer a lighter, even more portable solution. The monopod shown here is folded down for easy transport.

Monopods are not ideal for long exposures at night but are great if you need to shoot a fast moving subject with a longer focal length, such as a running child at a school sports day event for example.

Other Supports

It's worth noting that very basic digital cameras or those designed to be small enough to fit in a pocket may not have a way of connecting to a tripod. For these cameras you'll have to use an alternative means of support or use BluTack to 'stick' the camera to the tripod head. This is primitive but it works because such small cameras are very light. Make sure that you take great care that the camera is adequately fixed to avoid it falling.

One good alternative means of support uses a 'bean bag' construction which you can use to help cradle your camera on

fence posts, walls or even the ground. They're waterproof, come in various shapes and sizes and the filling provides a stable cushion into which you can snugly fit the camera. They're extremely versatile, as almost anything in the environment can become your camera's support. But again take care to ensure that the camera is securely supported.

Tripod Heads

The 'head' is the part of the tripod where the camera screws into place. Some use a special quick-release mechanism where the camera screws onto a mount that stays with the camera, enabling it to be quickly taken off without unscrewing it. More important, however, are the movements allowed by the head. Some tilt, some turn and some swivel all the way round, some do all three. The more movement you have, the more the tripod will cost, but the greater the flexibility once the camera is nestled neatly in place.

Using a Remote Release

To avoid exacerbating camera shake when you activate the shutter, you can use a remote or cable release. Some digital cameras accept a mechanical release that screws into the shutter button to allow you to take a picture.

Some use a special electrical release that works in a similar fashion but costs more. Other digital cameras come complete with a tiny remote control (as shown) that allows you to trigger the camera from another vantage point, including from within the shot.

Extra Flash

Almost every digital camera has a built-in flash unit designed to give a burst of artificial light, though they're so small that they don't always provide as much illumination as you need. But there are solutions for too little light.

Most digital cameras' flash units are ideal for subjects close to the camera or as a way of filling in shadows in brighter conditions, but not much beyond this. However, depending on the type of digital camera you own, you can increase the amount of light at your disposal by using an accessory or 'off-camera' flashgun. These are much larger and provide a much brighter, controllable burst of light than a camera's built-in flash. Several types are available.

Hotshoe Flash

Many digital cameras have a hotshoe on their top plate which is a secure fitting with electrical contacts. This provides a way to connect an accessory flashgun to your camera. Such flashguns have their own battery power (usually from four AA batteries) and once connected, an on-board computer 'talks' to your camera to get the flash exposure right each time it fires. This computer operates in the same way as it would for the built-in flash, and is automatically turned off when an accessory flash is mounted on the camera. Some

A D-SLR with accessory flashgun mounted in its hotshoe.

BUY A DEDICATED FLASH

While some, usually less technically complex, flashguns can be used on any camera they're attached to, they must be controlled manually. However, if you buy a flashgun made by the manufacturer of your camera or one made specifically for your make of digital camera, then they can provide 'dedicated' control.

Dedication is an advantage because the flashgun and camera work together seamlessly; the camera's metering and focus systems combine to help get better flash exposures. And such flashguns can also provide extra functionality such as stroboscopic flash (it freezes fast moving subjects) and finer control over the amount of light being used.

A ring flash such as this is designed for close-up flash work and can also be used effectively for portraits.

JUDGING FLASH POWER

The amount of light a flash produces, or its 'power', is rated using Guide Numbers (GN) and is measured at a specific ISO (light sensitivity) and at a specific focal length.

The higher the GN, the more powerful the flashgun. A GN of 11 is typical for most digital camera built-in flashes, and will provide enough light to illuminate up to around 11 feet from the camera, at a typical ISO (usually ISO 100) and a focal length of 50mm. A flashgun with a GN of 50 on the other hand will properly illuminate everything up to a maximum area 50 feet from the flash.

Note that if you alter the focal length or if you change the camera's sensitivity, the range a particular GN can illuminate will also change.

more expensive models offer comprehensive manual control.

Many flashguns also have what's called a 'bounce head' and these are the best types to use as the flash's head can tilt, turn and swivel in order to redirect (or 'bounce') the light at an angle. This allows control over where the light comes from, for example bounced off nearby walls or a ceiling. This is useful as it helps to increase

A 'typical' accessory flashgun showing the pivoting 'bounce' head on the top of a body that houses the controls and batteries.

creative opportunities (adding neat shadows over a subject for example by bouncing light from one side off a wall) or simply to reduce the harshness of the light hitting the subject if fired 'head on'. The more control and bounce

This flashgun is shown on a small stand for slave flash use. Note the data LCD on the back and many controls that provide all the functions needed to use the flashgun either as a slave or attached to the camera's hotshoe.

movement a flashgun has, however, the more expensive it will be.

Slave Flash

Slave flash units are another type of accessory flashgun, which can be triggered by detecting the light emitted by other flash units (or in some cases by using a special radio signal). As such, they are said to be 'slaved' to the main flash doing the triggering. In fact, you can trigger multiple slave flashguns simultaneously.

Some of the more advanced hotshoe flashguns can be used as slaves, but you can purchase 'dumb' standalone units too. Dumb freestanding units are inexpensive and can be placed almost anywhere but in either case, slaves are ideal for getting even more light onto a scene such as a very large room or a large group photo where one flashgun cannot cope on its own.

Studio Flash

Some high-end digital compacts and most D-SLRs have what's called a 'flash synchro' terminal. This is where a studio flash system can be plugged into, and triggered by, the camera.

Studio flash systems comprise large lights often with reflectors attached (they look like big umbrellas) and require mains power. Though they tend to be, as the name suggests, studio-based, some systems are portable and could therefore be used at home.

With such a system, you have ultimate control of the lighting of a subject, ideal for things such as portraiture. But they are very expensive and really only for the very serious photographer.

Extra Storage

Your PC may have a large hard drive seemingly offering plenty of space. But sooner or later you're going to need extra memory, so here's what you should look for.

Today's PCs come with large capacity hard drives, usually over 60GB. However, digital image files can quickly use up this space, as can the applications you use to work on those images. This will slow your PC down too.

External Hard Drives

External hard drives (or discs) are the solution to this. They are relatively inexpensive, simple to use and can provide you with an abundance of extra storage space - they're now available in capacities of over 500GB.

Onto these you can store your photos and any other large media files such as digital music files or videos you've captured on your digital camera. As a rough guide, a 100GB external hard disc can provide enough space for around 50,000 images, depending on their file size.

As with buying a PC, it's important to get as large a capacity disc as you can afford. Although seemingly more expensive at the outset, this actually works out much cheaper than buying several, smaller capacity discs, a situation you may find yourself in as your image library grows.

Once plugged into your computer, the hard disc will appear on your PC's desktop as a small hard disc icon and you'll simply be able to drag and drop onto it in the same way you can with other folders on your PC. They usually don't require any special software to install them and work automatically once plugged in. How to

actually store your data is dealt with in more detail in the topic *Backing-Up*.

Maxtor's One-Touch II Drive provides a simple to use desktop solution to image storage. As its name suggests, it's easy to use. When connected to your PC, one touch of its button saves images (or any data) across from the PC to its high capacity hard disc without needing any further intervention.

Speed and Connections

Regardless of what capacity disc you buy there are things to look for to help get the most out of your data and working environment. To start with, buy an external hard disc with at least a 7200rpm disc speed. Check the spec on the box before you buy or ask your retailer for advice.

Also, buy a disc with either USB 2.0 or FireWire (IEEE1394) connectivity but either way preferably with more than one port. Ideally, buy one with both types of connectivity.

This way you can be sure you have fast data transfer rates thanks to the connections, a high speed disc for quick data addressing (that's reading or writing your data) between your PC and the external disc, and you'll be able to 'daisy chain' multiple devices.

An example of the latter is having two external hard discs connected to one another and then to your PC, giving you more total storage. One external disc plugs into the other, and then that last disc is the one actually connected to your PC. Both discs will still appear as separate hard disc icons on your desktop.

Portable Storage

You don't have to confine extra hard disc storage to the desk at home or the office. Today there are a range of portable hard discs that provide you with extra storage capacity on the move, ideal for saving images from memory cards to free up space.

Many portable hard discs provide 'dumb' space, they're just a repository for the images and that's it. Others come with screens: some have large colour screens for image playback and browsing while others have black and white LCDs that just provide a simple way to check what's on the disc.

Top Left: Nixvue's Digital Album II is a stand-alone, palm sized, battery or mains-operated hard disc storage device designed for digital camera owners. It includes a memory card interface, push button copying of all your images to the hard drive, a remote control, slide show function and TV playback.

Top Right: The Elio Photo Jukebox is a compact size, high-capacity, portable hard disc and image player with a 20GB hard drive and 2.2-inch colour screen for image viewing and navigation. It can also play your digital music, it has an SD memory card interface for direct image downloading and special 'media management' software to help organise all the data stored on it.

The latest portable hard discs come with software built into them to play slide shows of the images. These can also be played on TV. Some can even play DVD style movies with sound, thanks to built-in speakers.

Portable hard disc capacities tend to be lower than their bigger non-portable cousins (between 20GB and 80GB) but still provide a compact high capacity storage solution, on the move.

You can also buy ultra portable external hard discs, which can fit in the palm of your hand or snugly in your camera bag. They are battery powered (usually a couple of AA batteries) with USB 2.0 connectivity so that you can connect to your digital camera or PC. Others have card slots so that you can plug in a memory card and transfer images directly from the card.

The Epson P2000 is a portable hard disc with a large, high resolution, 3.8 inch colour display that can show your photos, slide shows and even DVD-quality movies.

Light Meters

Still not getting the lighting right on your pictures? If you're suffering from pictures that are overexposed or too dark, using a light meter could be the solution.

A hand-held light meter may not seem to be an essential item given that all digital cameras have a built-in light measuring system of some kind.

However, built-in meters are sometimes not accurate enough, particularly for the demands of the enthusiast or professional photographer.

A light meter such as this one from Minolta has a white 'bulb' under which sits the light sensitive element used to measure light falling onto a subject.

How to Use a Light Meter

A camera's meter measures the light reflected from the subject, a person's face for example. A hand-held light meter can be used to measure this light as well but more importantly, it can also measure the light actually falling onto the face.

By holding a light meter alongside the subject, within the same light in which it will be photographed (called an incident light reading), you are able to assess that light more accurately. And that enables a more accurate measurement which can be used to hone your exposure setting on the camera. The reading from the light meter is transposed to the camera and you take your photo as normal.

To be successful, you need a camera with an all-manual mode where you control the aperture and shutter speed for example.

Most hand-held meters offer a range of sophisticated settings including a flash sync port (similar to that found on most D-SLRs) so that they can be used in conjunction with studio or off-camera lighting as well via a cable connecter (see *Extra Flash*).

Hand-held light meters can be expensive but offer a very accurate way to assess exposure and so can improve your creative potential.

Buying Guide

You can spend a lot on a high-spec multifunction light meter, but you don't have to. As long as you get a meter with the following features, it should serve you well.

Buy a meter that offers flash and ambient light readings. This allows increased control in all conditions.

Get a model with a sliding globe - a hemisphere of white plastic that can hide or reveal the meter's light sensor. This covers the sensor during incident readings or can be moved aside for reflected readings. A built-in sliding globe is safer as you won't lose it.

Look for a compact meter. Some meters can be quite bulky, usually larger models designed for studio use. Buy one that will easily slip into a shirt pocket or camera bag.

Consider buying a light meter with a flash sync port. You never know, you may end up using off-camera flash and with this capability built in, you'll be able to finely tune and control flash exposures, ideal in a studio environment for example.

Batteries & Power

There's nothing worse than getting ready to take a photo to find the 'battery low' warning flashing. Here's how to be fully powered up at all times.

The lifeblood of your digital camera, not all batteries are made equal. Here are some tips on getting the most from them and so your digital camera.

- Battery power is measured in mAh or milliamp hours. Only buy high-mAh batteries; 1000 mAh is better than 500 mAh as they have a higher power density and will last longer.

- If your digital camera uses four AA cells, you can save thousands of pounds over the lifetime of the batteries if you buy good quality rechargeable ones and look after them properly.

- Always charge your batteries properly, for the correct length of time. You can accurately determine the length of charge by multiplying the mAh figure by 1.4 and then divide that figure by the charger's current, indicated by its mA figure, which is usually displayed on the charger. For example, for a 2000mAh power battery, being charged by a 250mA charger, you would make the following simple calculation:

$$2000 \times 1.4 \div 250 = 11.2$$

So a charge time of 11.2 hours is needed. Failing to do this can reduce the life of the batteries.

Remember

Always take a spare set of batteries with you when you're mobile with your digital camera. Either charge up a spare set of rechargeable batteries or take new disposable ones along.

BATTERY TYPES EXPLAINED

- **Carbon Zinc**: Disposable batteries not suited to digital cameras.
- **Alkaline**: General all-purpose battery, cheap but not ideal for digital cameras.
- **Lithium**: Disposable and one-third lighter than alkaline batteries. High power, long life and environmentally friendly. Suitable for digital cameras.
- **Lithium-ion battery**: Some digital cameras come with this special battery 'pack' and charger, designed specifically for them.
- **Nickel Zinc**: Disposable battery similar to lithium in its good power delivery and low environmental impact.
- **NiCad cells**: Rechargeable batteries, not good for the environment but can be recharged for over 1000 charge/discharge cycles. Can suffer from the 'memory effect' which is a capacity loss if they are over- or partly charged, or not fully discharged before recharging. This means they cannot then hold a full charge or that they 'remember' their last, poor charge state.
- **NiMH cells**: rechargeable batteries that don't have memory effect problems, last a long time but are more expensive. Can be recharged over 1000 times.

Using Your Digital Camera

In this section, you'll find all you need to take great photos, including:

 How to use professional photo techniques – correct composition, focus and lighting

 Overcoming the common problems of low light, blurred images, poor framing, under and overexposure, washed-out colours and redeye

 Inspirational photo ideas to improve your creativity

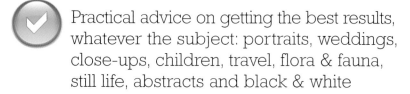 Practical advice on getting the best results, whatever the subject: portraits, weddings, close-ups, children, travel, flora & fauna, still life, abstracts and black & white

 Explanations of depth of field, exposure, white balance, F-numbers, ISO, shutter speed, aperture width, rule of thirds…

Composition

What makes one image more pleasing than another? By following a few simple steps about where to place elements within your pictures, you'll be surprised at how much you can improve your photography.

Composition is the name given to the combination of all the elements within the photo, and their position in the scene. Compositional rules can be thought of as guides to help get better photos. Here are some key techniques to keep up your sleeve.

Framing

Always fill the frame with your subject. If you are photographing a person, then make sure you can see them and that they are not too small within the frame. The benefit of this is that you make the most use of all the pixels you have at your disposal.

Another framing tip is to use frames within frames. When taking a shot, don't be afraid to use elements of your surroundings to frame a more distant part of the scene; shooting through a window including the window frame is a good example.

Portrait or Landscape?

Like any digital camera, yours can be used horizontally in its normal or 'landscape' position or it can be used upright in the vertical or 'portrait' format. While these names suggest the types of image you'd usually use each format on, experiment to see which works best for a given shot.

Rule of Thirds (or Golden Mean)

Using this 'rule', you can add tension and a dynamic 'feel' to your photos by careful placement of the main elements. First imagine that your digital camera's colour screen is split into a grid of nine equal squares; two lines running vertically and two horizontally across it. Depending on your digital camera, it may have the ability to display such composition lines on your camera's screen for you.

If you place the subject upon any of these lines or, in the case of positioning specific elements within a photo, where the lines intersect (these points are the so-called 'Golden Means'), the image can have more impact. Try placing the horizon across the top (or bottom) horizontal line rather than across the centre of the shot for example. Or place a person at one of the intersections when you want to put them in context with the background in a landscape-style photo.

Bull's Eye Composition

This is when the main subject of the shot is smack in the centre of the frame and should be avoided unless you have a specific reason for doing it. This type of image is less pleasing to the eye and lacks dynamism.

This shot of potters in Nepal uses the rule of thirds beautifully: both potters' wheels sit on the Golden Mean points. The graphic pattern created by the thrown pots adds interest, and energy comes from the use of a slow shutter speed that has allowed the spinning wheels to blur nicely.

Balance

You can create images with either equal or unequal balance. In the former you have elements within the photo balancing each side of the image, say two buildings of the same size. In the latter, you would have one prominent subject with another element in the scene placed on the other side of the frame that's either closer or farther away (whichever is best for the composition). Place a big tree one side, then a small rock or bush or person on the other for example. Although a subjective technique, it is one which can prove very successful when the elements are placed carefully.

Experiment

The last 'rule' and probably the most important is simply to experiment. Like so many rules, these simple techniques can be broken or bent and by mixing them you'll quickly learn how to get the best from your digital camera.

This image from the Namib Desert has a very dynamic structure thanks to the flowing curve of the sand dune and the sky. Colour is also very important here and the teeth-like effect of people walking on the dune's ridge adds both a sense of scale and energy to the composition.

Focus

Getting your images sharply focused is just a matter of pointing the camera at the subject and pressing the button, isn't it?

Focusing is critical to good photos and today's cameras usually have an auto focus system that quickly gets things sharp. However, not using this properly can ruin an otherwise perfect shot.

Most digital cameras have a central auto focus target indicated by a small square in the colour screen. Many use multiple focus points, which ensure off-centre subjects stay sharp. But, how many times have you taken a picture of family members side by side, with a gap between them and the camera has focused on the wall behind? Read on to find out how to prevent such problems…

If you don't let the camera focus by half pressing the shutter button and allowing it to focus properly, you'll get blurry pictures such as this shot of a baby.

Don't Rush the Shutter Button

All digital cameras that use auto focus have a dual pressure shutter button. A first, half-press-and-hold activates the focusing and other in-camera systems. There's a brief pause and then you'll get some form of focus confirmation: a green LED in the optical viewfinder and/or a green icon displayed in the screen. Only finish pressing the shutter release once you have these 'confirmations'. Trying to take a shot in one big press won't give time for the camera to set itself properly and you'll risk a blurred photo every time.

Portraits

In portraiture, your intention is to take a picture of a person. This usually means a head and shoulders shot or tightly cropped face, so always focus on the subject's eyes. If your camera allows control over which auto focus (AF) points you can use, select the

central AF point and use it to focus (half press the shutter button) and then recompose the shot, still holding the shutter button half way to preserve the focus selection. Complete the press to take the shot once you have the composition right.

Landscapes

To get a good landscape you need to ensure sharp focus from the foreground to the far distance. Begin by auto focusing on a prominent object in the distance. Haziness can hamper AF and if your digital camera uses a wide AF system ensure it does not set the focus to something nearby or at the edge of the frame. Then, keep the camera rock steady, using a tripod if necessary.

Use the camera's landscape scene mode –

if it has one – as this optimises the camera's settings for landscape work, or select a small aperture if using manual settings.

Macro Shots

Digital cameras offer some of their best results on close-up or 'macro' work. Some digital cameras can focus to within one centimetre of the subject, ensuring frame-filling shots of even tiny details. However, you need to ensure the correct part of the subject is sharp. Use a single AF point and recompose once it's in focus. Also use a tripod, which helps keep things stable if you have slow shutter speeds. Remember, for close-up work you can use the camera's macro mode or select a small aperture if using manual settings.

Small Groups

To prevent the problem of the auto focus locking onto the wall behind a group shot, either move the subjects to reduce any gaps between them, or focus on one person's face and then recompose. This way, you'll ensure that the group, and not the wallpaper, is sharp.

By concentrating the focus on the model's eye your interest is directed to her, the main subject of this reportage-style portrait.

Avoiding Auto Focus Problems

Some subjects always cause AF systems problems, so here are ways to avoid them.

- Parallel lines and regular patterns: These can be difficult for the AF to 'key' on. Try tilting the camera (from landscape to portrait for example), refocusing and then recompose for the shot.

- The dark: Unless your digital camera has an 'AF emitter' (it shines a beam of light out to help focusing), darkness or dark subjects provide nothing for the camera to focus upon. The answer is to get more light on the scene; turn on a light or two.

- Low contrast: Fog, haze, a predominantly white or black subject that doesn't provide the AF anything to focus upon can all present problems. You cannot change the weather; so try looking for an alternative but prominent element of the scene to focus upon. Also, use the camera's landscape mode, which ensures a small aperture is used.

- The Manual Focus solution: Alternatively, to help prevent any of the above problems, try using your camera's manual focus mode – if it has one. By taking control of the focusing yourself (check your camera's manual for operating instructions), particularly if you have the time to work on the photo, this will provide fine control and you can check the results on the LCD too.

Depth Of Field

The 'depth of field' is simply how large the focused area in a photo actually is. Let's see how it can be used to help create emphasis in your photos.

Everyone has seen photographs in which everything in the picture is crystal clear, from a foreground flower to the distant mountains. You've also seen pictures where only the main subject is sharply rendered, and everything else is blurry.

These are two examples of the effect which depth of field (DOF) can have. The former is a shot with a deep DOF (more of the scene is crisp) and the latter has a shallow DOF.

What is Depth of Field?

In more accurate technical terms, DOF can be defined as being 'the range of object distances within which objects are imaged with acceptable sharpness'. Thankfully, particularly if using a compact digital camera, you don't need to know the complexities behind the DOF calculations, just how to maximise it to your advantage.

So for simplicity, here are the key practical points about DOF:

- A wide aperture gives a shallow DOF
- A small aperture will give deep DOF
- A telephoto lens (or long zoom, at the 'zoomed' setting) appears to give shallow DOF
- A wide-angle lens appears to give a deep DOF

In points three and four above 'appears to' is used because while the perception in the shot is usually as described, it is not always - technically speaking - accurate. It depends on the subject magnification and scene perspective (or viewpoint) making direct comparison of focal length and DOF difficult.

However, although this may sound complex, you can now start to play with the DOF effect in your images.

When to use Shallow DOF

The most common use for a shallow depth of field is in portraiture where you want to emphasise the subject. By using either a long focal length on your lens and/or a wide aperture, say, F2.8 (see box opposite for explanation of F-numbers), you can get the effect of a sharp subject and blurry background. Use this technique on any shot where you want to separate it from its background. A shortcut is to use the portrait mode on your camera if it has one.

This portrait of a model at work had a very distracting background. A shallow depth of field has emphasised her face and blurred away the distracting background.

When to use Deep DOF

This is slightly more flexible but a good example of when to use deep DOF is for landscape photos. Typically, you'll use the wide-angle end of a zoom lens and a small aperture of, say, F8, which will help to ensure that the sharply rendered area in the shot stretches from near the camera to the far distance. A shortcut here is to use your camera's landscape mode if it has one.

Close-Up and DOF

It's worth pointing out that in close-up shooting, particularly if your camera has a good close-up or macro mode, the DOF will be very shallow indeed; a mere millimetre or two at most. Use a smaller aperture, F8 for example, to help deepen DOF if you want more of the small subject to be sharp.

Throwing the Background Out Of Focus

By selecting a suitable aperture, it is possible to throw the background out of focus by changing the depth of field. In the example below, the same scene was taken three times using different size apertures for each shot.

Firstly, a small, F16 aperture was used, which gives a sharp image from the gargoyle to the distant Montmartre in Paris. For the second shot, an aperture of F5.6 is used and now an element of blur has removed much of the sharp detail visible in the first shot. Finally, an aperture of F2.8 was selected and the background detail is almost completely blurred away.

The effect is to divert the viewers' attention increasingly to the foreground. This is in essence why control of DOF can be so powerful, particularly when there's a cluttered, distracting background.

USING F-NUMBERS

The physics behind the effect that aperture size or F-numbers (also called F-stops) have on photos is quite complex but here are some simplified ways to think about and use them.

The first thing to remember is that a low F-number of, say F2.8 gives a larger aperture while a high number, such as F8 gives a smaller aperture. A large aperture lets in more light and a small one less light.

Use apertures to:

Let in more light if it gets dark and you don't want to use flash or to get faster shutter speeds in brighter conditions. Here use a small F-number, say F2.8, to make a larger aperture until the exposure is correct in low light or the required shutter speed is achieved in bright conditions.

Control the DOF. Adjust the aperture to a small F-number (F2.8 for example) to get a big aperture and reduce the DOF (which will blur the background) when shooting portraits for example, or any shot where you want to blur backgrounds. Use a high F-number (F8 or F11) which will increase the DOF for close-up work or for landscapes and keep everything sharp in the entire photo.

Exposure

Exposure, the amount of light that reaches your camera's sensor, is the key to great photos. Here's how to control it.

Exposure is controlled by three elements: the camera's shutter speed, the lens aperture and the sensitivity. It is calculated by the camera's metering system for any lighting using a specific combination of these three elements. Alternatively, you can manipulate the exposure either to deliberately darken or lighten a scene, called under or overexposure.

Shutter Speed

The camera's shutter is a small, usually metal curtain that travels across the face of the sensor and helps control the quantity of light hitting the sensor. A fast shutter speed lets through less light, a slow shutter speed more. The faster the shutter speed the greater the 'freezing' effect it has on motion and vice versa.

Aperture and F-Stops

The camera's aperture is a small adjustable circular opening in a diaphragm within the lens through which light must pass to reach the shutter and then the sensor. The aperture's size can be varied (called the 'iris' control) and each position is called an F-stop.

The smaller the F-stop number the larger the aperture. The larger the aperture the more light is admitted. Aperture settings also have an impact on the depth of field (see *Depth of Field* for a fuller description of F-stops).

Sensitivity and ISO Equivalence

The digital camera's sensitivity to light can be increased, which is great if it gets dark. Digital camera sensitivity is based on a scale similar to that used for 35mm film sensitivity, called ISO and is typically 100, 200, 400 and upwards. The higher the ISO number, the more sensitive to light the camera becomes. (See *Low Light* for more explanation of ISO numbers.)

Increasing the camera's sensitivity (or its 'ISO equivalence') allows you to use higher shutter speeds or smaller apertures than would otherwise be possible at a given light intensity.

CAMERA TYPES AND LEVELS OF CONTROL

Being fully automatic point-and-shoot models, basic digital cameras will not offer any level of manual control.

Some mid-range models offer an aperture priority mode; you set the aperture while the camera sets the shutter speed according to your choice for a correct exposure.

Higher-end models provide control of both (aperture and shutter priority) where you make a selection of one, and the camera automatically sets the other to get a correct exposure. Some however, do offer full manual control, where both can be independently set by you.

Exposure Compensation

This is the ability to adjust the exposure by one or two F-stops (depending on your camera's sophistication), overriding the camera's automatic exposure control system and therefore lightening or darkening the shot. This allows fine-tuning of the exposure without adjusting any other settings and is ideal if extremes of light are 'tricking' the metering into under or overexposing.

Auto Exposure Bracketing

This is an automatic setting on more advanced digital cameras that carries out exposure compensation for you, automatically, and each time you take a photo. And it does it to a predefined level and on a predefined number of images, usually three.

Exposure bracketing means the camera takes one shot at the metered exposure, then (usually) a single underexposed and another overexposed shot as well. It takes these three shots (or more depending on the camera) each time you fire the shutter and you can pick the best shot to keep. The amount of under or overexposure can be preset by the photographer by up to one or two F-stops and again depends on the camera.

In this overexposed shot, note how colour has been lost and highlights have been bleached out making for an insipid looking picture.

An underexposed shot such as this one reveals plenty of colour but all the detail has been lost in shadow areas.

White Balance

Unlike the human eye, digital cameras can't automatically adjust to compensate for variations in the colour of light, potentially causing unnaturally coloured pictures. But here we'll show you how to adjust your settings for this – or use the effect creatively.

When shot with a digital camera, a candle produces a nice warm glow, normal household tungsten bulbs create a yellow colour and fluorescent strip lighting produces a cold-looking cast. Artificial light can produce such unnatural-looking colours because digital cameras are primarily designed to 'see' sunlight - that is light containing all the colours in the spectrum. They need to have their 'white balance' adjusted to take account of occasions when not all of the colours of the spectrum are present.

- Do use the correct WB mode for the lighting you're shooting in.

- Do use the auto WB mode if you're not sure of the light or if it's a mixture of various lighting.

Controlling White Balance

Most digital cameras are able to set the white balance for a given lighting in two ways. Firstly, there is an automatic white balance (WB)

This shot below reveals the difference that using the incorrect white balance will have on your photos. From left to right we have:
1 - Shade
2 - Tungsten
3 - Fluorescent
4 - Flash (the correct setting for the studio location)

- Don't worry if you get it wrong, change the WB setting and shoot again.

- Don't change the WB setting if you want to capture the mood the ambient lighting has created in the shot.

setting that adjusts the colours for you. Such WB settings can be found in the camera's set-up menus.

You will also find a range of possibly four or five other manually-selected settings in the WB set-up menu. These will include 'cloudy' (or 'shade'), 'tungsten', and 'fluorescent'. Some might have a 'mercury' setting and all will have a 'daylight' mode. Each setting alters the way the camera's sensor 'sees' and records the light according to the conditions.

Experiment with these settings outdoors and you will be able to see how each mode affects the image in the colour screen. Selecting tungsten for example makes daylight images go blue, as this is used to compensate for the warm colour cast attributable to household bulb lighting.

These settings more accurately capture and process the light than the catchall automatic WB mode, which entails extra processing of the image too. In other words, if you know the lighting you're shooting in, then select one of these WB modes so that you can fine-tune your shots. This will help get better quality shots and save time processing on PC later when you may feel any colour casts are too intrusive to the photo and need removing.

Creative Use of White Balance

There's one caveat to all this. Sometimes you might want to take a picture and keep the colour cast, for example when you want to capture the atmosphere the lighting creates, as shown here in the picture of the candle-lit church. In this case, the auto WB setting proved best, but experiment to see if you can get results that are even more creative.

Creative Flash

Your camera's built-in flash unit has more creative potential than you might imagine, it's not just for use 'in the dark'.

Most cameras automatically apply the flash when it gets dark or whenever more light is needed. Whilst useful in many scenarios, this can limit creative potential. By using flash in bright daylight you can add sparkle to a shot, reduce harsh shadows and boost colour too, so don't always think 'flash equals dark'.

Auto Flash

Most digital cameras' default flash setting fires the flash automatically whenever the camera's meter senses that the ambient light has dropped beyond a level at which a reasonable hand-held exposure can be made.

The flash fires every time in such conditions but the small size of the flash and the resulting flash exposure can leave the shot looking flat and dull, and you'll get unattractive dark backgrounds to each photo (see *Flash Fall Off* overleaf).

Auto flash is quite limiting, particularly if you want a photo that records both the atmosphere of a party and the people (see *Slow Sync Flash* opposite). So let's consider some alternative ways to use the flash.

Fill-In Flash

Fill-in flash, as its name suggests, is when the flash is used to fill in parts of the scene with extra light. It's 'forced' to fire each time, ideal for shots of a heavily backlit person or in situations where the camera's meter might be fooled by bright surroundings such as snow or on sunlit beaches.

This technique helps balance the

exposure between the flash and the ambient light. Altering the exposure is not always an option: exposing for the shadows in our portrait example here would have unacceptably overexposed everything else while a non-flash exposure would have left a dark shadow area on the subject's face. A puff of flash has worked a treat. Use this technique to add 'catch lights' in the subject's eyes too; it helps bring portraits to life.

To use fill-in-flash, turn on your camera's fill-in flash mode (if it has one) but if not, switch the flash to its forced flash 'On' mode (it will fire every shot) and the camera's metering system will do the rest. Some cameras will have an auto backlight feature to help out, automatically firing the flash when the background exposure level is much brighter than other parts in a scene.

Slow Sync Flash

Slow sync flash sounds complicated but in essence, it is just a means to synchronise the flash and shutter at a slow speed to help capture ambient lighting in a flash photo. The flash freezes any movement in the main subject while the slow shutter picks up the gloomier background. This is great for those shots where the flavour of an image comes from the ambient lighting – such as a party – but the people in the foreground are the main subject of your photo.

Most digital cameras will have a slow sync flash mode but if not, select a slow shutter speed and fire the flash (use the flash 'On' mode) and it will achieve similar results. Slow shutter speeds mean the camera will need supporting to reduce camera shake, although this can be used to creative effect if you want to add a dramatic dynamic to a shot.

Flash Off

Not strictly speaking a flash technique, it's here because there are times when flash is the last thing you want in a photo. These include taking photos through a window, or when taking photos of a flat subject or one with a reflective surface, where the flash would leave a 'hot spot' in the photo where the flash is 'bounced' back into the lens.

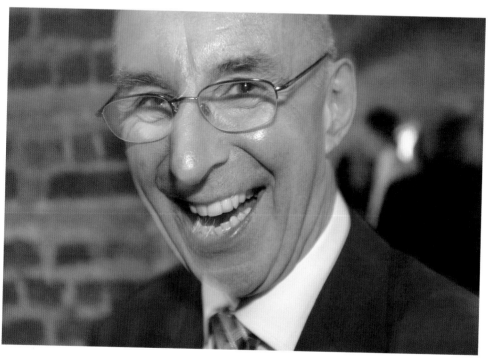

We have all seen photos of people taken with flash and they appear to have bright red eyes caused when flash light reflects directly back into the camera's lens off the eye's retina. It's red coloured because of the blood vessels in the eye.

Redeye is most common in low light (the eye's pupil enlarges to let in more light), and when using cameras where the lens and flash are close together - always the case on very small digital cameras!

Depending on the camera, whilst in redeye reduction mode the flash either emits a bright beam of light or a series of fast strobe flashes will fire. Both help reduce the pupil size of your subject, lowering the chance of light being reflected back into the lens.

Flash Fall Off

Flash fall off is caused by the flash illumination dropping off quickly beyond a certain distance. This happens because the intensity of illumination is inversely proportional to the square of the distance between light and subject. Put more simply, if the distance between light and subject is doubled, the light reaching the subject will be only one-quarter of the original intensity.

The result is that light for a correct exposure quickly drops away leaving backgrounds looking very dark, as shown here in our example picture. The man's perfectly exposed, but there's no detail in the background at all, even though this image was shot in a reasonably well-lit but very large room at a wedding.

To avoid this, try using the slow sync flash technique or use an accessory flashgun (if your digital camera has a hotshoe) to provide more light.

Low Light

Shooting in low light or darkness presents real challenges but can be one of the most rewarding photo techniques to get right. Let's look at the best ways to achieve stunning low-light shots.

Typical low-light photo scenarios include shooting cityscapes at night or shooting in a dark interior such as at a party, whilst still capturing the atmosphere created by the available light. Here's how best to shoot different dark scenes whilst avoiding the typical camera shake and image noise problems associated with low light.

Shooting At Night

Night photography, say a night landscape scene with the moon in the shot, presents a couple of key problems: keeping the camera stable is one and another is image noise (see right). A tripod or other such support will keep your camera steady. If you don't have a tripod then find a suitable wall, table or similar support on which to place the camera.

Ensure you set the largest aperture on your camera's lens (if you can control this feature on your camera) and turn off the camera's flash. Then set your camera's 10-second self-timer. This way, even if you jog the camera when you press the shutter button, the vibration this causes is gone when the shutter fires 10 seconds later. Select the camera's landscape scene mode, which ensures correct focus and on many cameras it will automatically deactivate the flash for you too. Also, try selecting the camera's night scene mode if it has one.

LOW LIGHT AND 'NOISE'

A potential Achilles heel that most digital cameras suffer, barring (to an extent) top-end professional models, is image noise in low-light shots. It looks similar to the effect of heavy film grain and is usually characterised by blue or red pixels peppering images shot in low light, particularly those with large areas of even colour. And the darker that 'colour' the more obvious and intrusive it can be.

Noise is created when the signal-to-noise ratio (the difference between the light captured, the 'signal', and the interference or 'noise' created by the camera's electronics, analogous to the hiss you hear if a radio is not tuned properly) is such that there's more noise than signal. Therefore a high signal-to-noise is good (think lots of light) and the reverse is not.

Increasing the camera's sensitivity (its ISO setting) makes the camera more sensitive in low light but has the drawback of adding extra noise. Try to stick with lower ISO settings, such as ISO 100 or ISO 200 and support the camera where possible. Also, ensure you switch on any noise reduction setting – if your camera has it. Noise reduction can extend the processing time between pictures; the worst effects of noise can be processed away.

Low Light and Flash

The night scene mode can also be used in low light. A slow shutter speed with a burst of flash records any ambient light and the flash illuminates the foreground. You still need to support the camera as a very slow shutter is used and the trick with the self-timer is a good idea too. Remember to use the camera's redeye reduction setting if the foreground interest is a person.

Night Portraits

Another common setting on many digital cameras is the night portrait mode. If it has one, select this mode when shooting people in low light. This will select a slow shutter speed combined with the flash – similar to that used in the night scene mode – but crucially, the flash exposure will be less powerful, helping to ensure the subject's skin doesn't bleach out, a problem if the flash light is too harsh.

Party Pictures

A perennial problem taking pictures indoors and particularly at parties is the relatively low available light. The flash will always want to fire and there's a risk of blurry pictures from camera shake if you turn it off because of the slow shutter speed.

Another problem here is that the small flash will not be able to cope with the areas you're trying to illuminate, even relatively small rooms can be too much for a built-in flash. The resulting photo will have a very dark background and this is called 'flash fall off'. The problem is surmountable by switching the flash to its slow synch mode (see *Creative Flash* for more on this). You risk motion blur, but this can, however, appear to be an intentional effect, as in the night-time shot here.

This shot was taken using the camera's night scene mode. The burst of flash has frozen the boy, but the background is blurred by camera shake.

This shot taken at ISO 200 has no noise problems, the image looks 'clean'.

An otherwise identical shot but this time taken using ISO 3200. You can see image noise is very obvious and seriously undermines its quality, filling the image with blue and red speckles.

CAMERA SENSITIVITY (ISO)

A camera's sensitivity to light is measured in ISO and the higher the number the greater the sensitivity to light. Here's an at-a-glance guide to ISO speeds and what they're good for.

- **ISO 100** (or lower): The best all round setting for bright conditions or where low noise is a key requirement.

- **ISO 200**: Ideal for slightly less bright lighting where low noise is still a requirement but not key.

- **ISO 400**: Noise might be an issue here on some cameras when printing at larger sizes. Provides faster shutter speeds in overcast conditions or low light.

- **ISO 800**: Noise will be evident even at 'normal' print sizes so use the camera's noise reduction if it has it. Ideal where fast shutter speeds are needed to freeze fleeting action.

- **ISO 1600** (or higher): This setting will only be available on high-end digital cameras and professional D-SLRs; it offers very fast shutter speeds in very low light. Noise issues are as above, but high-end models will have special noise reduction algorithms to reduce this.

Close-Ups

Close-ups are one of the most practical and creative areas of photography and a real strength of digital cameras. Here's how to make the most of your camera's macro abilities.

Close-up or macro (its technical term) photography opens new perspectives on our natural world and most digital cameras are very good at it. Even basic models have macro modes built-in enabling this great technique to be used without needing specialist equipment.

Digital cameras are good at macro because they have a combination of small sensor sizes and short focal length lenses. Together these provide closer focusing distances than would otherwise be available with 35mm film cameras.

Some can even focus as closely as one centimetre – that means the subject can be almost touching the lens. Even if your digital camera doesn't have a macro mode, as long as you can focus the camera sharply on subjects within 20cm of the front of the lens (or closer) you can shoot good close-up shots.

How To Take Close-Ups

Just like a 'normal' photo, when shooting close-ups the subject appears in the camera's LCD, which you use to compose and focus your subject properly. If your camera has it, select its macro setting as this helps get focus spot on, and gets metering and depth of field (DOF) to the optimal level for the shot too.

A drawback is that macro results in very shallow DOF so you will find that just a very

---

IDEAS FOR CLOSE-UPS

The practical and creative uses for macro shots are almost endless, so here are some simple ideas for you to try.

- Photographs of your jewellery or stamps in a stamp collection can be shot in close-up for insurance purposes, as well as being attractive images in their own right.

- Garden flowers make stunning subjects and are easy to find and…

- Insects such as bees and butterflies, which you'll find on those garden flowers can also look great in close-up.

- Textures and patterns often look dramatic in close-up too. If it looks bad 'big', think small and close in for a macro shot, it may just be worth it.

MORE MAGNIFICATION

One way to get greater magnification if you cannot focus really close is to shoot from further away, zooming in to get a closer crop. You can then use software on the PC to crop closer still later. But this means you lose pixels (you've cropped them away) so you won't be able to enlarge the prints as much. Zooming in will also reduce the DOF.

small area is sharp and the rest of the subject will be out of focus (see the poppy shot example) so you may need to shoot several pictures until you're happy with the focus point. Adjusting the aperture to use a smaller F-stop (F8 for example) will help deepen the DOF but will result in slower shutter speeds, so you may need to use a tripod to steady the camera in order to prevent camera shake.

Subjects such as butterflies or jewellery make for good shots, but insects tend not to sit still for long, so timing is everything. Practise on static subjects such as in our example here – of a pair of cufflinks – where you can control the focus and lighting and your subject is not likely to fly away!

This shot was taken using the camera's macro setting and focused on the stamens. Note the shallow depth of field.

Avoiding Flash Problems

Because the close focus distance on most digital cameras is very close indeed, using the camera's built-in flash will either not illuminate the subject at all or the lens will get in the way and cast a shadow over it. Natural light offers an even lighting over the whole subject, but artificial light from a table lamp is also ideal as you can set the camera's white balance to take away any colour casts (see *White Balance*). If you want to use flash, then you may need to use an off-camera flashgun, if your camera can use one. These can be positioned away from the camera, angled to give the best effect for creative shadows or angled for all-over lighting - whichever you want to use.

Black & White

Black and white photography provides another creative weapon for your digital photo armoury and it's easy with today's digital cameras. Here's how.

Almost all digital cameras have a series of black and white or monochrome ('mono') modes within their menus that provide a host of easy ways to get more creative with your photography. Monochrome simply means the camera uses only one range of tones to make an image, so everything in a picture is shown in shades of just one colour.

Different Monochrome Modes

The black and white mode is the most popular mono mode, used to add a certain arty flair to otherwise mundane photos.

Sepia is another popular mode that mimics the look of an old faded photograph. It uses a range of brown tones to create an image with an 'antique feel'.

The document mode is another useful mono mode. This is primarily used to shoot documents, as you might have guessed, where you want to make sure the wording is clear and crisp by creating a very high contrast mono image.

Thinking in Black and White

Shooting colour is one thing, but a successful black and white shot requires just a little more thought. Although you can still shoot anything in black and white if you wish, what looks good in colour will not always lend itself to this approach. But it is ideal for capturing texture, form and shapes, as these can look better with the more graphic representation that black and white offers.

Good subjects range from stark, winter tree lines, rocky mountains, landscape vistas or close-up images of textures such as stone, wood or the walls of buildings. Look out for these and the small details that may stand out to make that 'graphic' look in the shot. Try to imagine it in black and white. Pick the best angle to exaggerate the lines or rugged bits and it should provide the right look in the shot.

If shooting people, remember to look for those graphic elements such as a craggy, characterful face, or the mood created by shadows, which all help to give the image the

Textures are an ideal subject for black and white photography, as this driftwood on a beach reveals.

turn from colour to a greyscale image; that is, an image that has all the colours represented by a range (or 'scale') of greys, from black all the way to white. This is helpful as it lets you see how the image will look when you shoot it in black and white.

Be warned that some colours will look identical once converted into black and white. Yellow and blue end up looking the same, for example.

It's worth noting that even very basic image editing software can perform the same sepia or black and white trick on any colour image on a PC, and we look at just this technique in the topic *Creating Black & White*.

Think laterally, as in this shot taken from a light aircraft. The sky, wing, sea and clouds combine for a great graphic effect in black and white.

right feel. It takes a little practice but once you've taken a few successful black and white shots, switching from colour to black and white will become almost second nature and you'll know just by looking what will look good and what won't. When shooting sepia shots, it's best to try and frame the subject so that modern paraphernalia, such as lamp posts, telegraph poles, cars and pylons are excluded. This helps keep a timeless look and makes the old fashioned sepia look work more successfully.

Practical Advice

Use the camera's LCD in the mono mode of your choice. When you switch your digital camera to its black and white mode, either from its relevant menus or the control assigned to this task (check your camera's manual), you'll see the image in the LCD

Even common or 'in-the-garden' subjects can lend themselves to black and white, so you don't need exotic locations.

Portraits & People

Taking pictures of people sounds simple enough, but there are key ways to make sure these precious photographs do their subjects justice. First, we'll have a look at the basics, and then move on to some great ideas and tips to make your people shots really stand out.

The Basics

The most common problem with people pictures is 'amputation'. How many times have you seen photos with a person's head mysteriously cut off or their feet missing?

This is very easily avoided with a digital camera as you can see everything in the LCD screen exactly as it will appear in the photo. Always use the LCD to help you compose correctly: you will be able to see if you have got it wrong, and can delete the shot and try again.

Another basic trick, if you're *not* doing a close-in portrait, is to put the person in context. This is ideal if you're shooting a candid style image of someone working for example. Rather than cropping in tightly, shoot the subject in their environment to 'tell a story' with the photo.

Don't be afraid to photograph people small in a scene, allowing more of the background in. This gives space around the subject in the shot, and is ideal if you want to convey a sense of scale.

Formal Portraits

A formal portrait is any portrait where the shot has been deliberately set up, as opposed to a candid shot (see overleaf). However, formal portraits don't have to look posed – you can still get your subject to pretend and set up the shot to look like you've caught someone behaving naturally. For any type of pose to be successful, you need to try to relax your subject and get them to be themselves. Try to get a rapport going.

The classic formal head and shoulders crop, where you compose so the subject is cropped across the shoulders just below the collar line, is effective and looks clean. But you don't have to stick to this. Full body portraits can be equally as effective, particularly if you want to convey a character trait such as flamboyant clothing.

- Look for character and emphasise it, such as a craggy, lined face or flamboyant clothing.

- Remember to focus on the eyes.

- Use a long focal length, around 100mm can be ideal. This will also help by removing distracting backgrounds.

Above: Candid portraits can work well if you can capture the person unawares. Here the woman has relaxed, seemingly 'drifting away' as her hair is being styled.

Lighting

If shooting outside in daylight, getting enough light is not an issue, but if shooting indoors the quality of lighting will play a big part in the success of your people shots.

CANDID PORTRAITS

Candid or 'informal' shots of people are probably the most common type of picture you'll take, and include anything that's not posed. To capture a good candid, you'll normally be shooting on the hoof, without a tripod or stopping to 'set up'. Roam around to look for unusual angles or just to capture spontaneous or emotional moments.

A classic environment where candids work is at a wedding. The subjects are usually relaxed, unaware they're being photographed, and you're left to snap away to your heart's content. This spontaneous style of people picture is increasingly being used by professional wedding photographers for just these reasons.

To take a successful people picture, you must think about what, who and how to shoot. Use a focal length suitable for the effect you want: telephoto for longer focal length shots to remove distracting backgrounds; wide lenses for group shots and where you want to include the background of the scene. And don't limit yourself to upright format shots; landscape format images can work too.

If you intend to photograph a stranger, you should be courteous and ask their permission before you snap away. While it's not always possible to do this, it can make the situation more relaxed, so you'll have more time to shoot and get a better snap. If the person poses making the shot look awkward, ask them to ignore you while you shoot for a more natural picture.

Clearly, your camera's built-in flash or additional lighting can help here (see the topics *Extra Flash* and *Creative Flash*). However, a simple way to get a great lighting effect is to use natural light streaming in through a window. It'll be diffuse and provide nice soft shadows. However, if the light is too bright and shadows too harsh use a white sheet of paper or card to reflect light onto the face's shaded side as a 'fill-in'.

If you are using flash and the exposure is harsh, lower the flash power (if you have the flash exposure compensation function on your camera) or switch to fill-in flash. Or just turn the flash off and use the available light, remembering to adjust the camera's white balance accordingly to stop unsightly colour casts (caused by indoor artificial lighting).

- Don't be afraid to 'grab' a shot. If a scene presents itself in a fleeting moment, go for it. You can always just delete it if it doesn't work. You never know!

- Always fill the frame; don't waste a pixel anywhere.

- Don't forget to 'think in black and white'. Your digital camera's black and while mode can make the difference on a grey day or if the person in the shot would be great photographed this way, at a historical event for example.

- And last but not least, don't be afraid to experiment.

Above: Portraits that are formally posed can be very effective. Use of light and shadow here has given the shot 'mood' as has the sitter's characterful face.

Still Life

Still life photos capture everyday objects in a way that can make even the seemingly mundane look beautiful – if handled well. Check out these tips for making the 'still' come to 'life' with your digital camera.

'Still life' is defined as photographing inanimate objects, and can include almost anything, from flowers in a vase, coloured beads, sliced fruit and vegetables to ornaments and objets d'art.

When shooting still life, you need to consider both the subject and the surroundings. You'll need to think about how you arrange your subject, where you'll place it and then how it will be lit.

Composition

Pay close attention to the subject's arrangement. Don't place objects in a line for example, as regimented composition rarely works well. Stagger your subjects – but not at equal distances from each other – and if you have to have them in a row then overlap them.

Then try to shoot from an unusual angle such as directly overhead or from very low down. Remember to think about the background. Neutral backgrounds work well, and can be provided simply by a draped cloth. But you may want to include some of the surroundings. Try it and check what looks best in the camera's LCD.

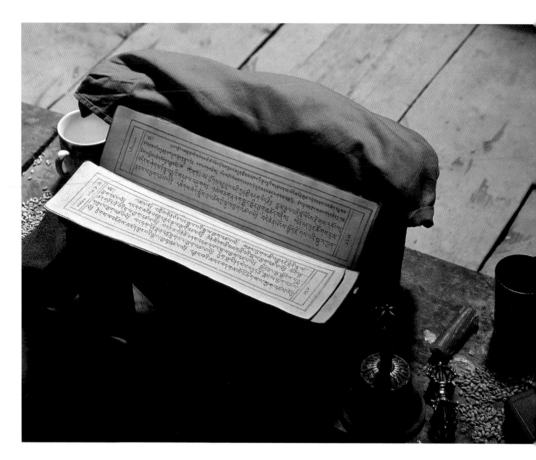

Opposite: These flowers make a stunning still life image. Note how natural light from a window, controlled by curtains to create shadow, has been allowed to fall across the flowers, which stand in a vase on a simple, plain wooden floor. Also note the depth of field is quite shallow, helping to keep attention on the flowers.

Above: This is a classic still life image, shot in available light, of a Tibetan monk's scripts and robe shot in situ at a monestary. Again, the background is out of focus due to a shallow depth of field, keeping the viewers' attention on the main subject.

Lighting

Still life subjects tend to be on the small side, so lighting is important. Using your camera's built-in flash may be adequate for this but if it lacks a flash exposure compensation function, the light it emits may be too harsh and could also create a heavy shadow.

Additional off-camera flash can be helpful here, and you can also exercise more control over this. The light from a flash gun can have its angle adjusted (by bouncing the light with a bounce head flashgun for example) or be softened with a diffuser. Diffusers are accessories usually supplied with a flashgun that fit over the gun's lamp to soften ('diffuse') the light. If you don't have one, a simple piece of tissue or tracing paper placed over the flashgun's lamp will be just as effective.

If you don't have a flashgun, it's not a problem because natural light from a window is also ideal for still life. A good idea is to leave a slit in the curtains allowing a stream of light to flood across the subject. This works really well for glass, coloured or otherwise, and any reflective subjects, where the spectral highlights (the bright, reflective parts of an object) are enhanced and add sparkle.

Alternatively, you can use any suitable table lamp (or even include them in the shot if they're attractive or ornamental) and reset the camera's white balance accordingly. Try the trick of using white card to act as a simple reflector, or aluminium cooking foil to help get dazzling reflections and shadows falling where you want.

As you'll need to use longer focal lengths in more subdued lighting, your camera may need the aid of a tripod or some other support to avoid camera shake. Longer focal lengths also affect the depth of field so use your camera's aperture control (if it has one) to adjust this as needed.

- Use natural light from a window or artificial light and adjust the camera's white balance to compensate for any unwanted colour cast.

- Use white card or paper as reflectors to help control the light and shadow on a subject.

Below: This image shows a typical mundane subject that can still make for a stunning still life image. The table top makes up the background thanks to careful framing while control of the depth of field focuses attention on the coffee beans in the cup. Natural light from a window to the left (you can see it reflected in the saucer) keeps unwanted reflection to a minimum.

Above: Tomatoes cleaned and lit with bright natural light are a simple but effective still life composition that anyone can try. The light has been judged by spot metering from the tomatoes, not the bright background.

Right: A superb still life of jewellery taken using natural light on a white backdrop. This is also a classic use of creative control of the DOF.

- Don't use regimented lines of subjects, stagger them or allow them to overlap for a pleasing composition.

Reportage

Reportage - using your digital camera to tell a story in a series of pictures - is one of photography's greatest uses. Here are some inspirational ideas for projects, and tips on getting the best results.

Project Ideas

Almost anything can be given the reportage treatment, but family events such as an important birthday or birth of a new baby are of course very popular choices. If you've ever taken a series of photographs of guests enjoying themselves at a wedding, then you've already tried reportage.

They needn't be one-off events, however. You can just as easily keep a photo record showing how your children grow up, from newborn baby onwards, which would become a fantastic memento. Or maybe you want to record the progress you make as you redecorate your house or work on some other long-term practical or creative

endeavour. Projects such as these are the essence of reportage.

Enthusiast photographers might want to tackle more ambitious projects such as changes in their community or home town as it's redeveloped. To make this easier to cover, you could follow the developments in just one part of your locale or the changes to a famous building for example.

Another good subject to follow is a local historic event. You could even find that your 'documentary' work, particularly if it's comprehensive, can become a valuable social document that local museums or historic societies would be interested in.

In the example shown here, the photographer was asked to capture and

 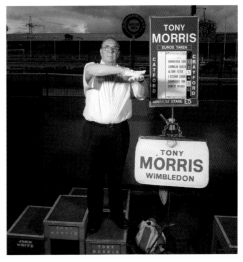

- Store the photos carefully by date but remember...

- Because your photos are digital, the date and time of each photo is embedded in each shot and can be read on a PC, perfect if you can't remember when a picture was taken.

- Take many pictures and try to cover all the 'angles'. It doesn't matter if you 'waste' shots – you can always delete the ones you don't need later.

- You may want to re-shoot the same place time and again, over many years in some cases, and from the same viewpoint, so use a tripod and be patient.

- Shoot at regular intervals, once a day or week, dependent on the subject you're following of course.

- Keep a diary of events if photographing something that will be a long-term project. Using your PC it would even be possible to combine your words and pictures and print out your own 'publication' on the project.

- With long-term projects, you really don't want to take any risks with all the work you've put in. So don't keep all your images on memory cards alone. Make sure you back them up to your PC or other external memory device (see *Backing-Up*).

explain the hand signals used to transmit betting information to and from trackside bookmakers in greyhound and horse racing. His aim was to show the different signals the bookmaker uses as the betting progresses.

The four shots shown here are just part of an extensive selection that formed a dictionary of bookmakers' gestures used in a national newspaper. You'll need to give your subject a similar 'sequential' treatment.

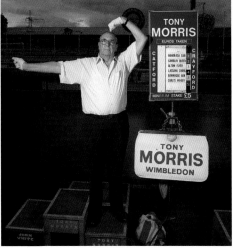

Travel

Travel to foreign climes often presents photo opportunities that will never come your way again. Make sure you make the most of these once-in-a-lifetime images by following these inspirational ideas and our practical travel checklist.

From the Plane

If you're flying, there's usually an opportunity to get some stunning images from the aircraft. You won't be able to carry loads of photographic kit into the cabin of course, but even a simple digital camera with zoom lens can get good shots. Use the telephoto end of the lens to exclude the porthole in the shot, or go with the wide-angle end of the lens, as in our picture, to include it as an extra framing device. Look for shapes and patterns in the cloud – or on the ground – and you'll have a good chance of shooting a breathtaking image before you've even arrived at your destination.

Local Flavour

When away from home, it's always nice to capture local flavour. Unusual buildings and architecture make eye-catching images that can tell the viewer where you were in a single shot. But also look out for other elements of the locality. If you travel to an exotic location, don't just shoot the mountains or the local scenery, get shots of the locals too, particularly if there's a festival or local event. This shot, taken at the Jaipur Festival has captured dancers in traditional clothing.

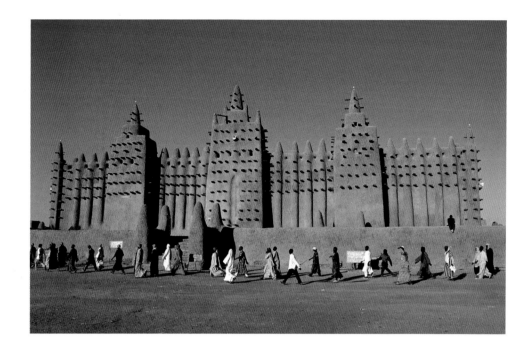

The Early Bird

Try to get up early on holiday, particularly if you travel to a country with a very hot climate. Early morning light is often the best for any photo. And if it's very hot, the heat of the day creates haze and dust, which can lower contrast, reducing your photo's impact. Another advantage of being an early riser is simply, with the sun lower in the sky, you get better shadows, ideal for enhancing landscapes. The same is true for landscapes shot later in the day at sunset though light tends to be warmer at dusk than dawn.

Sunset Shots

A beach holiday abroad can often provide stunning sunset shots (right), but then so can a trip to the mountains. Either way, one sunset can look much like any other unless you try to include something extra in the scene. To get spectacular beach sunsets include other foreground interest, perhaps someone standing at the water's edge (using the rule of thirds to place them, the horizon and the water lapping the shore). Alternatively, use palm trees arching into the shot to create a 'frame' for the sun. Even beach huts can add interest and give the sunset a 'place'.

Away from the beach, the options are usually more obvious – mountains in the distance for example – or once again, a person placed carefully to 'balance' the composition. Experimentation is the key, but remember that low light could mean you need to use a support for the camera to stop camera shake.

TRAVEL PHOTOGRAPHY CHECKLIST

- Unlike film cameras, digital cameras and their memory cards are NOT affected by airport x-ray machines, but always carry your camera as hand luggage (rather than checked into the hold) so you can shoot from the plane's portholes.

- Carry spare memory cards or a portable storage device to free up space on your memory card. There's nothing worse than running out of memory as a great shot presents itself.

- Take a support of some kind, even a small, table top tripod is better than nothing if you need to keep the camera steady for a crucial shot.

- Spare batteries are an absolute must, particularly if you're travelling to a country where getting hold of replacements is going to be difficult. If you use rechargeable batteries then remember to take your charger *and* a travel power adapter.

- Protect your camera from excessive heat and dust. Never leave it in the window of a car in the sun and always keep the camera in a case. You could even buy a waterproof housing which will help protect the camera not just from water but also from dust and sand.

Architecture

Architectural photography is rewarding but also very challenging. It can even be hard to do justice to famous buildings that offer potentially stunning results. Here's how the professionals do it.

Architectural photography can include anything from churches, castles and monuments to bridges and sculpture, so there's plenty to choose from. Whatever your subject, there's a natural temptation to try to cram the whole building into one shot and that urge should be held in check. It *can* work on some buildings but it's often not successful.

Less is More

If you don't have a wide enough lens to take in a whole building from where you stand, you may have to step so far back in order to force everything into the shot that there's no visible detail left. In addition, you can end up with clutter in the foreground that can ruin the shot.

The telephoto end of your digital camera's zoom lens is the solution here. You can use it to crop in close for a more detailed image and you'll quickly find that, with architecture, less is often so much more. Look for the little architectural details that will make an interesting image. Alternatively shoot only part of the building in context, revealing some of the background.

In this way the building will still be recognisable, particularly if it's a famous structure, but you get a unique view of it that can add interest to an otherwise bland or well-known façade.

Exaggerate Perspective

Exaggerating perspective can work really well with tall buildings by shooting them from a low angle, particularly if you have an interesting or clear blue sky. In the tall building image shown opposite, the buildings have been shot to exaggerate the converging verticals, and the clouds in the blue sky balance the composition.

Go Black and White

Don't forget to try out your digital camera's black and white mode. This can work really well on older buildings or where a modern building lends itself to the 'graphic look' that black and white so often creates.

- Use the wide-angle end of the lens (that's around 35mm or wider) or get a wide-angle adapter for your lens to help get broader views. Alternatively, use your camera's panorama feature to stitch many shots together on your PC.

- The telephoto end of your zoom will enable you to crop in closely on a detail if you can't, or don't want, to fit in the entire structure.

Above: Using a wide-angle lens from a low viewpoint has worked well on this shot; the sky balances the two buildings compositionally too.

Change Your Viewpoint

If it's at all possible, change your viewpoint. Some buildings provide access to towers, balconies, basements or viewing platforms – utilise these whenever you can. It will add interest and once up (or down) there, other interesting shots will become apparent.

Shoot vertically up the wall too, but if you try the reverse of this – from a high vantage point looking down – make sure you always have the camera attached to you via its carry strap. Look for natural frames such as an archway or go for reflections in lakes or ponds, all can make excellent alternative views of buildings.

Bridges can be so huge that you have no choice but to stand well back to fit everything in. Again look for details and perspectives that offer a new and unique shot. For example, go to the river bank or try to shoot down the length of the bridge to get a receding perspective of the structure.

Above: To fit all of this building into one shot would look very 'busy'. But in this shot, closing in using the zoom lens has helped to give a sense of scale, show detail and make for a superbly graphic shot.

Night shots

Another professional's tip is simply to shoot at night. Even stark or uninteresting buildings can take on a completely new personality at night. A tripod or other support will be needed to hold the camera steady. Also, it's best to survey the building during daylight so you'll already have an idea of the best angles and views.

Shooting Statues

Statues can make excellent subjects but involve extra considerations. First, because statues tend to be relatively small, there's a danger of underexposure as there's usually a large expanse of bright sky behind them which fools the meter. Switch the metering to centre-weighted or spot to ensure the

metering is from the statue not the sky behind.

Walk right around statues to look for the best shot or to see if there's a better background. Try to balance the shot with other compositional elements such as trees or parts of the background to 'set the scene'.

- Watch out for underexposure particularly if there's a bright background. Use centre-weighted or spot metering.

- Avoid clichéd shots - move around to find a unique view, particularly of famous monuments or buildings.

Landscapes

Landscapes are ideal images to grace any wall. Here are a few ideas on how to make them as striking as possible.

The single most important thing in landscape photography is to get up early to catch the morning light. Why? Because morning skies are clearer. A lack of haze in the atmosphere produces a better quality of light, and you get raking shadows from the lower angle of the sun which is a good effect. That established, here are more expert tips to improve your landscapes even further.

Below: Here the tree in the foreground helps to guide you into the shot, and without it the image would be ordinary. Also note its positioning using the rule of thirds.

Leading the Way

One of the best ways to make a success of a landscape shot is to have elements placed within the composition that lead the viewer's eye into the shot. Anything in the foreground such as a plant or rock, then a tree in the middle distance and then, perhaps, a distant hill all help.

A swooping hillside with the ridge running across the frame and receding into the distance works well, or even rows of crops in a field that all run into the distance or up the side of a hill. Once the viewer's gaze is drawn to the distant part of the scene, it helps to have another element sitting there waiting: a building, tree or even an interesting cloud formation on the horizon.

Framing the Picture

Don't be afraid to have things intruding into the shot at the top and sides. The idea is to frame your landscape with something actually in the scene; tree branches just hanging into the shot across the top edges for example. The combination of the photo's shape and the other 'framing' elements help to draw the viewer into the scene and add interest. This so-called 'frame within a frame' technique can work well but practice and experimentation is needed to see what works best.

Rule of Thirds

The rule of thirds can make a huge difference to a landscape shot (see *Composition*). All the elements of your composition can be brought together in many ways, but by placing key elements using this rule, you can make an

- Get up early to capture the best of the early light.

- Shoot at the highest resolution your camera has and its highest quality (compression) settings.

- Use small aperture settings (larger F-stop numbers) to ensure narrow depth of field.

- Use a shutter speed fast enough to freeze any potential camera shake.

- Or support your camera on a tripod or other prop. Keeping your camera rock steady is a good way to ensure sharp landscape shots.

CORRECT SETTINGS

Your digital camera has a finite number of pixels to employ on any image, but with landscape shots, it's vitally important to use every single one of them and to use them at the highest quality setting. This is because detail in a landscape shot can be tiny in the frame, perhaps only one or two pixels across, particularly if it's a distant part of the scene.

So select the camera's highest resolution possible. Then select the camera's highest quality mode. These usually run from 'Standard' or 'Good', through 'Better' or 'Fine' to 'High Quality' or 'Best'. Check your camera's manual to be sure you have picked the best settings in all these departments.

White balance should be set to the conditions: Sun for bright sunlight, Cloudy for cloud and so on. If you're not sure then stick with the Auto setting which will be adequate in most cases.

Use a small aperture (a high F-stop number such as F8) to make sure the depth of field is narrow, and set the camera on a tripod or other support to keep it steady – or make sure you use a shutter speed fast enough to freeze any potential camera shake.

even stronger composition. Experimentation is important here – shots that don't work can easily be deleted. Sometimes it even helps if the rule is broken.

The Right Format

Just because it's a landscape shot, you don't have to use the camera in its landscape or horizontal format, with the longest edge across the top. Portrait format works as well, depending on the subject. Some of the images we've used here are upright shots that would not work as well with a 'wider' perspective. You can check both options in your LCD.

Left: In this shot, the foreground grasses guide your eye into the shot, the ridge on the sand dune takes it in further and the deep blue sky adds dramatic colour contrast.

Above: This shot of the San Juan River uses the curve of the canyon, the shape it forms and dramatic clouds to help create a stunning image. Here the rule of thirds has been broken so the interesting sky can become a key part of the scene.

Overleaf: The upright (or portrait) format has worked well to emphasise the leading lines created by this shot of a road. The sky has been given the top third of the frame with the road filling the entire foreground. The white lines and telegraph poles help add further dynamism to the shot.

Sports & Action

Capturing the action with a fast-moving subject such as sports can be a real challenge. But with a few key tips you can shoot the fastest of fleeting moments to dramatic effect.

Sport or action photography can include everything from photographing super fast sports cars, your child running at their school sports day or your dog jumping to catch a ball. In short, it's any shot of a fast-moving object which can be difficult to shoot sharply.

Helpfully, even the most basic of digital cameras has some form of 'sports' mode that can help capture these moments. But here are some additional techniques that will help you avoid blurring or even completely missing your subject.

Panning with the Subject

One way to help get shots with a sharp subject and blurry background is panning with a moving subject. This involves watching the subject in the LCD (or viewfinder) as it moves and judging the right point to capture it.

Stand with your feet firmly planted and smoothly swing the upper part of your body as the subject moves across and in front of you and, as the subject hits the point you want to take the photo, fire the shutter.

Previous page: In this shot, a fast shutter speed of 1/2000th second and large F3.5 aperture were used to ensure the action was completely frozen. This aperture has allowed plenty of light to get to the sensor and helped blur the background slightly.

Above: For this shot of washer women in Mali, a shutter speed of around 1/30th second and panning with their motion helped give the shot a dynamic feel.

Shutter Lag

Many digital compacts however, are affected by shutter lag. This means that there's a short time delay between pressing the shutter release and the shutter actually firing. This is no problem for standard photos but in action shots this delay means you risk missing the subject completely.

Basic digital cameras suffer the most from this. It's caused by the on-board computer taking time to focus, set the metering and generally get the camera primed to take the photo. More advanced cameras have faster processing and so suffer less from this problem. The best way round this with a basic model is to use a pre-focus technique.

Pre-Focusing

This technique solves the problem of shutter lag because you pre-focus the camera at a predetermined point. Set the camera's focusing system to manual and focus it using the chosen point. If you don't have a manual focus setting, find the point you know the subject will pass, and half press the shutter button to focus on that point. Then, keeping the shutter half pressed, follow the subject, pressing the shutter the rest of the way when the subject gets to the right pre-focused point. This will give a sharp action image with a blurred background. Use the same techniques but without panning to get a sharp subject and background.

Slow Sync Flash

Another idea to try is slow sync flash. Here, a slow shutter is combined with a burst of flash. The flash freezes the subject motion and the slow shutter speed keeps the background blurred. It's the same mode as used in low light, but can be equally creative in daylight.

Timing

Timing is everything, particularly the timing required to catch the subject at the right point in the action. Practice makes perfect, but whatever the subject take plenty of photos. Set your camera to shoot continuously, which is usually around three frames per second. Some can shoot more, some less, depending on their sophistication.

If the camera has a sports mode it will do all this for you. Just keep the shutter button pressed and it will just keep on taking pictures until you let go.

What Focal Length?

You'll find that a longer focal length is best for capturing sports or action shots where you cannot get close to the subject. Racing tracks or stadiums are good examples - you've probably seen the banks of sports photographers at sporting events using huge telephoto lenses. You'll need a digital camera with (ideally) a 10x zoom lens or use a D-SLR with a 250mm or longer lens.

Longer focal lengths mean slower maximum shutter speeds particularly if it's gloomy. Watch out for camera shake, increase the sensitivity (ISO), which helps get faster shutter speeds, and open the aperture to a larger setting (a smaller F-number) such as F2.8.

PROFESSIONAL ACTION TIPS

- Use a fast shutter speed to freeze the action. The faster the subject is moving, the faster the shutter speed will need to be – around 1/250th second or faster. Increase the ISO (sensitivity) if required, but only bump it up to that needed to get the right shutter speed.

- Use slower shutter speeds to add 'creative' blur. Not all subjects lend themselves to 'freezing' and might look more dynamic if there's a little motion blur in the shot. Speeds slower than around 1/30th second are best in daylight but a smaller aperture (higher F-number) might be needed to stop overexposure.

- Flash can help freeze action but you'll need a flashgun with plenty of power and a camera with a hotshoe to accept it.

- Use a slow shutter speed at night to get action blur such as car light trails or funfair rides 'streaking'. Speeds of around 1/10th second or slower are good depending on the amount of 'streaking' you want.

Left: Slow shutter speeds can be used to capture light trails from cars or, as in this case, a funfair's Ferris wheel, shot with a shutter speed of around eight seconds.

Weddings

Getting stunning shots at a wedding can be tricky. But there are some simple steps you can take to ensure that this most important of days is beautifully and safely recorded.

Be Prepared

The key to successful wedding photography is preparation and planning. You need to get organised: visit the venues beforehand, talk to the bride and groom so that they're relaxed for the photos on the day, and plan out what shots you'll need to keep everyone happy.

A professional photographer can easily rack up over 200 shots at a wedding, so if you're planning to cover the whole event, ensure you have plenty of suitable capacity memory cards available - or a way to back photos up such as a portable hard drive. Also check your camera is functioning properly, your batteries are charged and you have any necessary accessories to hand.

Group Shots

Group shots can be difficult to coordinate but one way to achieve good groups is to watch what the professional photographer does and take the same shots. But you must make sure you don't get in their way or in their shot.

Big groups will need the wide-angle end of your camera's lens, then zoom into the group as it gets smaller. If you can, shoot each group with different backgrounds. Control depth of field with the apertures (F-stops) and use larger apertures to blur the background. Keep checking the shots on the LCD to ensure they work, and if not, take them again.

Above: A classic 'bride getting ready' shot taken at home before the service and the sort of intimate image that helps sum up the day.

Candid Shots

Candid shots are a great way to capture the spirit of a wedding in the way formal, posed shots don't always allow and such informal shots are also easier to take. Catch relaxed people chatting and happy figures enjoying the day. Also, look for closely cropped shots of faces, and target the small animated groups that congregate at a wedding. Don't be afraid to use unusual angles or the camera's black and white mode.

Shots in the Church or Venue

Flash will be almost essential indoors. But it's even better if you use a support such as a tripod and slow sync flash to give an ambient exposure that will capture both the people and the atmosphere. If in a church, check whether you're allowed to shoot inside and if you can use flash. It's unlikely you'll be able to shoot during the ceremony.

Above: Another idea is to shoot aspects of the bride's or groom's outfits. This shot of a bride's shoes on a windowsill using only natural light was taken while she was getting ready.

Below: Don't forget the bride and groom's more intimate shots after the group photos; this one has been taken using the camera's sepia setting.

ESSENTIAL SHOTS CHECKLIST

There are a number of traditional shots you'll need to take at a wedding:

- The bride at home: including preparations, and individual and group shots of the bride and bridesmaids.

- The groom arriving at the church or venue: don't forget the best man and ushers, the groom's parents and other immediate family.

- The bride's arrival: don't forget the bridesmaids, and waiting to enter the church or venue.

- Inside the church/venue: ideally a tripod shot (it'll be dark) to capture the atmosphere.

- Signing the register: the bride, the groom and a group shot with witnesses if possible.

- Walking down the aisle: including the happy couple outside the church or venue with guests swarming round and the crucial confetti-throwing.

- Groups: if you are arranging this, do the biggest groups first so that some guests can then depart to the reception, leaving more time for shots with the bride and groom. So start with big friends and family groups, then the bride and groom with the bride's family and the groom's family, followed by closer family and the bridal party, and finally intimate portraits of the bride and groom.

- Entry to the wedding reception, followed by cutting the cake, and the toast with glasses raised, being clinked together.

Opposite: The black and white mode on your camera is ideal for candids such as this shot of a demure bridesmaid. The gentle blurring is deliberate and helps give the shot a softness, ideal for the subject, and was achieved by using a slow shutter speed.

Right: This type of slow sync candid image at the reception is fun and simple to take.

Gardens & Flowers

Photographs of gardens in bloom or individual flowers can make stunningly colourful photos. With these ideas, the flowers in your garden can be made to look just as beautiful as any botanical garden.

Lighting

One of the key aspects of flower photography is careful consideration of the light. Although bright, direct sunlight brings out the colour, it's also very harsh and creates deep shadows. Often you'll find an overcast sky can provide the best lighting, particularly if you're shooting close-ups. Flash, while available to you, is not always ideal as it can 'blast' so much light onto the flower that it bleaches out the detail and colour.

A great tip for controlling the available light is to use pieces of card. You can use them to shade a close-up shot from direct sunlight. White card can be used to reflect flash (if using an accessory flashgun) or to reflect available ambient light to fill in shadow. Alternatively, you can deaden 'hot spots' with black card. You can also use the card as a backdrop, helping remove a cluttered background from a shot of a single bloom for example. Try the same shot using either white or black card for a different backdrop in each shot.

Close-Ups

The close-up techniques already discussed (see the topic *Close-Ups*) are particularly effective with flowers. You can really use the camera's macro power here. Don't just shoot the entire flower head, get even closer and shoot the detail of stamens or even just the veins in the leaves or petals, if your camera can get that close.

You'll need to fill the frame. Remember to use a small aperture (high F-stop number) to increase depth of field and use a shutter speed that will not only stop any potential camera shake but also freeze the flower if it's windy, typically a speed at least equal to the reciprocal of the focal length in use. Don't forget those bits of card, they come in handy as a wind shade too. If you have a tripod or other camera support, use it for even more stability.

Wider Vistas

As with landscapes, you need to think about composition when photographing a vista of plants: the shape of flowerbeds can be important, as can ranks of plants with the same colour. Zoom in and out of the shot to see if a smaller part of the scene looks better or offers unusual patterns that would be missed with a shot of the entire area. Move your viewpoint constantly and look for the best angle or vantage point.

Shutter speeds should be kept fast enough to stop camera shake and motion blur and at least equal to the reciprocal of the focal length in use. However, one technique is to use motion blur to your advantage, particularly if it's windy and if there's a field of swaying flowers or corn for example. Set the camera on a sturdy support, and use a small aperture and slow shutter speed to catch the motion of the swaying plants. The result should be a sea of attractively swishing plants that will look like brushed cotton or a beautiful smoothed surface.

Getting Creative

Avoid the temptation always to stand up when shooting flowers. Changing your point of view even just by dropping to your knees can have a dramatic effect. If you want to emphasise a single plant or bloom in the foreground with a distorted perspective, lie down and use the wide-angle end of the

zoom lens. Focus on the foreground flower – it must be close to the lens – and you'll have an (apparently) giant bloom or plant in a wide, distorted landscape. This is very effective if you choose your bloom wisely – a single prominent plant is better than a larger bush for example.

Again you can use your pieces of black and white card, along with a water spray bottle. Use the spray to add a mist of water droplets to the flowers and plants. This adds fantastic 'freshness', mimicking morning dew for example and this also catches the light, making even boring plants look more succulent and attractive.

Below: Filling the frame works well if there's a cluttered background. You may get a more interesting interplay of form and colour, such as in this close crop of crocuses.

PRACTICAL CHECKLIST

- The basic approach is to shoot the entire flower or flower bed to fill the frame.

- Use a household water sprayer on blooms and leaves to add attractive highlights which help make the flower look crisp and fresh.

- Don't ignore other elements of gardens such as interesting fountains or buildings. Each may be worth a shot on its own or to give contrast to the plant elements of the scene.

- Hunt for the best blooms. Look for blemish-free flowers; you don't want anything that has marks or brown patches.

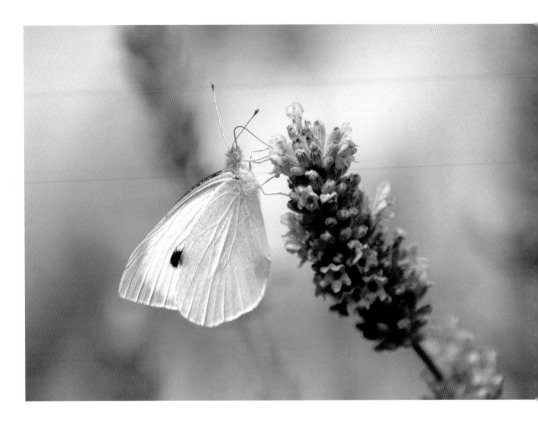

Opposite: A windy day doesn't have to stop your creative flower photography. Here, a slow shutter speed and metering from deep within the poppy head overexposed the background and gave the shot 'creative' blur.

Above: You can combine flower photography with close-up work and get great results like this shot of a butterfly on lavender.

Right: If there's any architectural interest or features use them to your advantage. Here, a backlit fountain has been shot with a fast shutter speed to freeze the brightly sunlit spray.

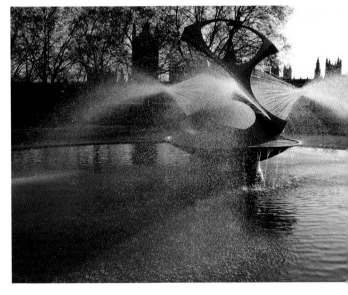

Children

Children are understandably the most popular photographic subject. So make sure you know how best to capture those childhood moments for posterity.

From newborn infant to graduate, children are in front of the lens for most of their lives. Despite this, getting great shots can be a challenge as children rarely stand still and will get bored when you want a more serious or studied family portrait. Here are some ways round this.

Babies

Newborn babies offer plenty of scope for creative as well as fun shots. For instance, a close-up of a baby's hands (or feet) juxtaposed against an adult hand can make a moving image. Such shots will require a close zoom and should ideally be taken when the baby's asleep, unless they're particularly relaxed after a feed. Use natural light for a charming softly-lit image.

Other ideas include portraits with the happy mum and dad where the baby is held proudly cheek-to-cheek, and shots with the baby cradled lovingly across a parent's chest. However, avoid a full body shot while the baby is sleeping, particularly a shot from above as this can look dull and lifeless, especially if harsh flash is used. If you want to shoot a full body image, get down to the baby's sleeping level and close in. Use soft natural light from a window and the image will look full of life, relaxed and natural.

Opposite: By constantly looking and waiting for the right moment you can get wonderfully wistful shots, as with this natural light shot of a little girl.

Toddlers

When babies are starting to move around, real fun can be had. Set your camera to its sports mode if it has one or use a fast shutter speed. Try to get in on the action; if they're playing on the floor lie down with them. If you want a vibrant shot, get colourful blankets and dress them in bright clothes. If you use flash, watch out for dark backgrounds generated by flash fall off. However, this might be desirable in a portrait image for example.

If there's more than one toddler, then drop to one knee or lie down to get on their level. Zoom out and try to capture their play. A slower shutter speed can help here – motion blur can make things look both active and humorous. Don't forget the camera's slow sync mode where a burst of flash can freeze the children's play whilst the slower shutter captures the ambient atmosphere and some movement too.

Parties

One of the most challenging child photo opportunities is a party. Try to get a fun shot of the whole group – get the other parents involved if needed. For slightly older children, get them all to pull a funny face in one shot, and a serious face in another. Making more of a game of the photography and showing them the results on the camera's screen often means they'll want to do more photos. But work as quickly as you can.

At the party table, you must of course get the candles-being-blown-out shot and use

slow sync flash for the best effect. You'll also need to shoot all of the children seated at the table but it's usually hard to fit everyone in as it's unlikely you'll have a wide enough focal length. In this case, shoot from one end of the table and try to get the kids to lean in – ensure you get every face. If you have room stand on a chair and shoot using the wide-angle end of your zoom lens. Get someone to hold the chair and be careful.

Younger children will often not cooperate for such shots so the best technique is to move around looking and waiting to get the 'moment', snapping as you go. Look for small groups of two or three children and you'll eventually get all of them this way. Remember to keep the children on side by continuing to show them the pictures on the camera's LCD.

Growing Up

Photograph the key moments in your child's life, everything from the first tooth appearing, starting at school, being a bridesmaid or pageboy to college graduation. The photo techniques used will depend on the moment and atmosphere you want but keeping a record of such momentous events can build into a wonderful album of images or a PC slide show (see *Creating Slide shows*). But remember to back up all these priceless images (see *Backing-Up*).

Above: Intimate shots such as this baby's hand can work well in both colour and black and white and when juxtaposed with a parent's hand for example.

Opposite: An unguarded moment for these children at a wedding has been captured well. The timing is great as the young bridesmaid has just realised the shot is being taken.

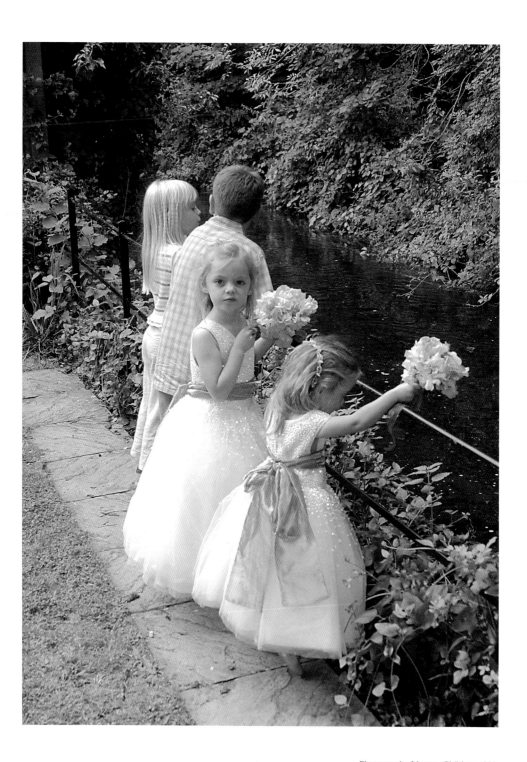

Pets & Animals

Photographing animals and pets can be very tricky but the following tips will help you get prize pictures of all different kinds of creatures.

Basic Techniques

Pets can be treated just like any subject when considering the photo techniques involved. All the elements such as composition, exposure and focus must be right. Focus on the eyes, compose the shot so the animal looks 'natural' and set the camera to its portrait mode for posed-style shots. Use the sports setting if you want to get photos of a dog jumping around in the garden for example.

Accurate exposure can be problematic, as all-white or all-black animal coats can fool the metering and under or overexpose. Check the results on the camera's LCD and adjust the exposure (lower or higher shutter speeds for example if you have manual control).

Flash

Like humans, pets can suffer from redeye although in animals it's often bright greeneye! Use an off-camera flash to avoid it if you have one. If using a camera's built-in flash unit, use the redeye reduction mode and, if indoors, turn on more lights. This will help reduce the animal's pupil size, cutting down the chance of greeneye. Remember however, that flash can startle an animal, so use natural light whenever possible.

Timing

One major source of frustration will be getting your pets to stay still once you point the lens at them. Timing is everything. You'll need to be patient and watch the animal playing, poised for *the* shot. A squeaky toy can come in useful here to get moments of alertness as they play or start to slumber.

Alternatively, recruit a helper, someone able to occupy the pet and keep it lively. However, you'll have to try to keep them out of shot to keep the photo looking natural. Move around searching for the right angle as the helper encourages the pet to sit or play as you want it to.

Zoos and Safaris

Photographing animals in zoos can be difficult as the cage may get in the way. Use a large aperture (lower F-stop number) and a long zoom, and focus on animals further back in the cage. The resulting narrow depth of field means the fencing should be practically invisible in the shot.

If you're on a safari or travelling to see other animal life in the wild, the most important consideration will be your lens. You're unlikely to be able to get close to the animals you're photographing, so a long zoom is essential, the longer the better. Some of today's 10x and 12x zoom compacts are ideal for this and if you own a D-SLR you'll need a lens with at least a 300mm focal length equivalent.

Opposite: For humorous shots, use a wide-angle lens setting to exaggerate the shape of an animal's face. Be sure to focus on the eyes though.

Left: If you can't get a shot of an animal in action, go for detail or colour, as in this striking portrait of an owl at a summer fete.

Opposite: This shot of a cheetah was actually taken through cage bars. Using a large aperture and long focal length of 200mm gave a shallow depth of field ensuring the cage didn't intrude into the shot.

Left: This resting, but alert, dog just needed a little help to prick up its ears. A quick whistle from the photographer did the trick.

TIPS FOR SHOOTING PARTICULAR ANIMALS

- For dogs and cats, the best bet is to give the animal something to play with, such as a squeaky toy or a bone if it's a dog. This takes their mind off the camera but you'll have to be ready to trigger the shutter quickly.

- Shooting fish in a tank can be tricky as you need to avoid reflections from the glass (or water if the fish are in a pond). Avoid flash and get the lens as close to the glass or water surface as possible (you may need to switch on the camera's macro/close-up mode for small tanks). Wait for the fish to pass by the lens or to stop moving.

- For smaller pets such as hamsters, mice or guinea pigs getting close enough can be a problem. The best solution is to shoot them in someone's hand. Use the camera's close-up mode and fill the frame with the animal. If the animal is in a cage, use a larger aperture as the narrow depth of field will help to ensure that the cage bars aren't visible.

- For sea life, many digital cameras can be used underwater with a special, waterproof housing, ideal when snorkelling. You'll need to get close to the subject and the lower light underwater means a higher sensitivity setting (ISO 400 or greater) should be selected. Flash presents a problem as a phenomenon called back scatter means light is bounced back into the lens from particles in the water, ruining the picture. This can only really be avoided by waiting until there's less muck in the water or more available light.

Abstracts

Abstracts are the potentially stunning and unusual patterns in a landscape or scene, from large-scale cloud formations to the small-scale geometries of grains of sand. Our tips will help you search out the best abstract shots.

The human eye is tuned to look for patterns in everything we see. It's the reason our ancestors could 'see' constellations in the heavens: we love to find order in seemingly random things. In photography the trick is to spot these patterns and then crop the image properly to achieve the effect you can see. Depicting a subject with the thrust of the shot aimed at internal structure or form, rather than the thing in its entirety, can make shooting abstracts very gratifying.

Inspiration for Abstracts

Abstract patterns occur in almost anything: shadows, freshly mown grass, wooden fencing, leaves on the floor, a multitude of illuminated windows in a building at night or even people milling about a railway station, but abstracts from nature are the most common. To shoot any type of abstract successfully, you have to think about what you're seeing in terms of shapes and forms (in a similar way to how you must think in black and white when snapping mono shots). For example, a macro shot of a flower can unveil an interesting cell pattern on the leaf, which then becomes a striking image in its own right.

Man-made objects can provide inspiration too. Perhaps take a tight crop on a manhole cover that shows its stippled surface and dirt or rust. Either zoom in or, simply, move closer to the subject and use the wide-angle end of the lens. Both approaches will provide an abstract shot with an 'industrial' feel.

Colour and Abstracts

It's not just shape and form that can create an abstract. Looking closely at colours, and patterns of colours, will help too. An abstract can lurk anywhere within a colourful vista - markets are great examples of this, as our image of colourful shoes shows. Perhaps an easier example to find would be a selection of ties hanging on a shop rail? But remember colour is as important to the look of an abstract as the form of the subjects themselves.

Above: Regular patterns can help form abstracts as can colour, but here both combine - in rows of colourful new shoes - to produce a great abstract image with strong form. Note the use of an unorthodox angle; the shoes have been photographed to exaggerate the perspective of the racks in which they lie. A flat 'straight on' shot might work but not as effectively as this.

Using Angles

Another tip to help get abstracts from seemingly mundane subjects is to change the angle from which you shoot. Even tilting the camera so it is composed neither landscape nor portrait but diagonally can help, and may provide a better frame within which the abstract will work. The shot here of shuttered windows provides an example of how looking for other angles can be used to produce unusual shapes and form in your images.

Below: Looking around you at unusual angles can present photo opportunities. Here the shuttered windows, narrow confines of the buildings and overexposed sky all contrive to make a pleasing 'form' abstract.

Large-Scale Abstracts

If you are flying, grab the chance to shoot from a completely new perspective. The shot opposite of white clouds over the red-looking desert is a classic, large-scale abstract. The clouds start the whole composition. A tight, zoomed-in crop helps exclude all but the colour of the red earth below which is vitally important to the composition, and keeps a graphic feel. Best of all, the shadows formed by the clouds add a 3D feel to the shot. But you don't have to shoot from an airplane to obtain large-scale abstracts, they can exist anywhere. You just have to look for them.

Opposite: Large-scale abstracts can be found when flying, like this stunning image of clouds and their shadows floating over the red earth.

Below: Without looking down, the photographer would have missed this shot of pots drying in the sun in India. To catch abstracts you need to look around you and really see what's there.

ABSTRACTS CHECKLIST

- Zoom in, zoom out, move closer, and move away. A seemingly boring leaf on the floor might become something else entirely if you move in to capture the pattern of its veins, or zoom out to include all its fallen fellows on the ground.

- The subject you're shooting will dictate the exposure parameters you need to use, but don't be afraid to experiment. Assess the results in your LCD then try another approach.

- A trick to see abstracts more easily is to look through the camera's viewfinder or its LCD to see if a shape or pattern presents itself that is not immediately apparent otherwise. Try it and it might just surprise you.

- When shooting close-up, look for the finer patterns within the subject.

- Think shape, shine, form, colour and scale.

The Digital Darkroom

In this section, you'll find all you need to digitally enhance photos on your PC, including:

- How to use editing software – finding your way around programs, using tools and menus, and saving to the different file formats

- Basic digital techniques – autofix, cropping, straightening, resizing, sharpening, brightening, redeye removal and converting to black & white

- Advanced techniques – using colour management, levels, curves, channels, cloning, dodge and burn, masks and layers

- Masterclasses – the professionals' way to blur backgrounds, add movement, make panoramas, restore old prints and apply special effects

- Explanations of JPEGs, TIFFs, GIFs, PICT, PDFs, filters, RGB, image editing tools...

Starting To Use Editing Software

Image editing software allows you to manipulate your digital photos on a PC, from simple corrections to complex special effects. First we'll introduce you to finding and using the editing functions.

Image editing software comes in many varieties, from the basic tools included with your digital camera to the highest level of software designed for imaging professionals and true enthusiasts.

The software that comes on the CD-ROM with your digital camera is okay for basics such as resizing and modest corrections to colour and image size, but for the majority of editing tasks, as found in this book, we recommend you buy one of the many off-the-shelf image editing packages available (see *Which Software?*). With these, you'll have a powerful editing tool for just about any image editing task you can think of.

Throughout the image editing topics of this book we will use examples from a very popular consumer-level editing software package, Adobe Photoshop Elements 3. As it's a typical package, you should be able to achieve all the effects described in this book, whatever commercial software package you are using.

Finding Your Way Around

Though there are lots of different image editing packages on the market, all of them use very similar tools, and editing functions. They'll even have very similar workspaces, with the main tools ranged down one side (usually the left side though you can move them around). Across the top, an 'options' bar

provides ways of changing individual tool settings (such as brush sizes) and access to other menus with even more choices.

Helpful hint windows or 'wizards' are often incorporated into the software, and these will automatically pop-up when needed to assist you with simple editing techniques.

Tools and functions can be accessed in a number of ways: through menus that appear (or 'drop-down') when you click on them in the options bar; in a small window that pops up on the desktop; or by clicking on an icon (a small picture that indicates a function). Usually, if you hover the mouse cursor over an item for a moment (without clicking), its name will appear over the tool so you can always check what it is if you're not sure.

While your software will have all or most of these menus/tools, the names and locations may differ depending on the package, so always read the manual that comes with your editing package or use the on-screen help assistant in the program to search for a particular function.

What follows overleaf is a list of the key tools from the most popular software packages so that even if the names vary, you'll know which tool icon to look for.

Menus and windows you could find on your desktop

Options bar
When an image is open, the options bar will be displayed across the top of your workspace. It provides extra settings and controls for whatever tool you have active at the time.

Menu bar
Major functions can be accessed by clicking on the relevant command on this bar to access a drop-down menu.

A drop-down menu
A typical drop-down menu accessed from the menu bar. In this example the 'enhance' menu is offering options to adjust the lightness of the image via the levels command.

Tool bar
Clicking on an icon will activate the relevant editing tool (see overleaf for a key to tool icons).

A drop-down menu
Menus can drop down from selections on the options bar. One of the most useful is the brush menu, shown here, allowing you to select the type of brush you want to use.

A window or 'pop up'
These pop up on your screen to provide choices when their associated function is selected, often from a menu. In this example, an options box accessed from the levels menu has popped up.

Tools Explained

Marquee Tools: Used to outline a selection in an image for copying or cutting.

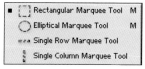

Lasso Tools: Used to surround specific objects in an image in order to select them for cutting or copying for example.

Healing Brush/Patch (not available in all packages): This tool samples pixels from one area and copies them using the texture of the pixels from a selected area to 'heal' marks such as spots in a portrait shot for example.

Clone Tool (or Rubber Stamp): Allows the copying of pixels from one area to be pasted over another area.

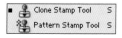

Eraser: As the name suggests, this is used to remove/erase pixels from an area in an image.

Blur/Smudge Tools: Tools that allow you to blur or smudge pixels.

Path Selection Tool (also see Pen Tools): Allows you to draw a selection around objects in an image that can then be removed. Paths can be saved for use on other images.

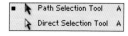

Pen Tools: Allow you to draw, create and adjust 'paths' around objects in an image.

Crop Tool: Allows you to define an area in an image so that you can permanently 'crop' away the rest.

Hand Tool: This tool allows you to move an image around in an open window if, say, you've magnified the image and want to see an adjacent area without altering the magnification factor.

Foreground Colour (a): This allows you to define the colour of the foreground in a layer.

Background Colour (b): Clicking this lets you define the background colour.

Exchange Colours Tool (c): Works with both the Foreground and Background Colours (above) to swap quickly between the two.

Default Colour Settings (d): Clicking this resets the colour of the foreground and background to their respective black and white positions.

Display Mode - Standard: Sets the software to display the images in the standard edit mode.

Display Mode - Quick Masks (not available in all packages): Sets the software to display the images in the Quick Mask edit mode.

Screen (Display) Modes: This controls the way images are presented within the workspace: maximum size for example.

Move Tools: Allow you to pick up and move elements within an image or on layers in a document being edited.

Magic Wand Tool: Allows you to quickly select (or make a selection of) all the pixels of a similar colour to the ones clicked on.

Brush Tool: Selecting this tool activates the brush currently active in the Brush Palette.

Selection Brush Tool (not available in all packages): Paints a selection (or Mask in Mask mode) onto an image or layer.

Pencil Tool: As the Brush Tool.

Gradients Tool: Allows you to apply predefined gradients across an image or layer.

Zoom Tool: Magnifies an area of the image you're working on.

Paint Bucket Tool: The paint bucket allows you to fill (or 'pour') a chosen colour into large areas of an image (or selections) without the need to 'paint' it in by hand.

Dodge Tool: Mimics the traditional darkroom effect of lightening part of an image by reducing the 'exposure' of those pixels.

Burn Tool: Mimics the traditional darkroom effect of darkening an area of the image by increasing the exposure of those pixels.

Type Tools: These tools allow you to apply text into an image or layer.

Shape Tools: These draw custom shapes into an image on a separate layer or layers.

Colour Samplers: A pipette style icon for a tool that lets you 'sample' colour from pixels for use elsewhere in an image or layer.

Saving Your Photos

If you adjust images on your PC and don't want to lose your work, you need to save those changes. But there are various ways to do this - here's how to pick the best one for any situation.

Save/Save As

You have two main saving options: 'save' and 'save as'. The first overwrites the existing data with your changes, in other words you lose what was there before and it gets replaced with the new, edited data.

The second option lets you save the image as a new file with a new name of your choice. In this way, you preserve the original file as it was and create another image file that has had the changes applied. This is ideal should you make a mistake, as you can go back to the original file and work on it again and 'save as' again.

While the latter means you double up on files – you'll end up with two files; one edited and saved and the other original, left untouched – it also allows you to retain the original files for future use and for archiving (see *Backing-Up*). So now let's look at the commonest file formats available, for you to use in most image editing programs.

File Formats

Digital images are created by your digital camera using a range of special data structures – or formats – that allow them to be 'seen' by a variety of programs on PC. Each format has advantages and

disadvantages that may mean you prefer one type over another, depending on what you want to do with the finished image.

Each time you save an image, you need to decide which file format to use. Some formats save the image using compression, which is a special computer algorithm that crunches your images down to fit into a smaller memory space.

Some compression algorithms remove data to do this and are called 'lossy' formats, here data is 'lost' in order to 'squeeze' (or compress) the file. Other formats offer compression without losing data or creating artefacts, and these are called 'lossless' formats. The amount of compression is nowhere near as high as with 'lossy' formats, but you'll still be able to reduce the file's size by around 50%.

JPEG or JPG Format

JPEG (denoted by the '.JPEG' suffix or sometimes '.JPG' depending on the camera, program or PC you use) is a lossy format and can be compressed down to around 10% of the original file size with slight loss of quality. If a file is saved using JPEG compression, the JPEG format looks for similar pixels and removes those that are not needed, then it makes a 'best guess' to put them back again when the file's opened, say on a PC screen. It is for this reason that small errors in the compression algorithm can cause a drop in quality as occasionally it gets those 'guesses' wrong. This compression process can also create JPEG artefacts, small blocks of unwanted pixels in the image.

You can save JPEGs at settings between 1 and 10, with one being the lowest quality (most compressed) setting and 10 offering the highest quality, least compressed file. A setting of five or six usually provides the ideal balance between file size and quality for most uses.

```
Photoshop
BMP
CompuServe GIF
Photoshop EPS
✓ JPEG
JPEG 2000
PCX
Photoshop PDF
Photoshop 2.0
Photoshop Raw
PICT File
PICT Resource
Pixar
PNG
Scitex CT
Targa
TIFF
```

This is a typical save menu in image editing software indicating the various file formats you can choose to save the image. JPEG is highlighted with TIFF at the bottom of the list.

TIFF Format

TIFF (denoted by the '.TIFF' or '.TIF' suffix) is a 'lossless' format and is the best file format to choose if you need to maintain the image's quality; memory space is not an issue; and you don't want to compress the file as heavily as you might with JPEG. TIFF stores information about colour and dimensions as a 'tag' appended to the file (and hence the name: Tagged Image File Format) and is the standard file format to use for saving high quality images ready for printing for example.

Photoshop File Format

Photoshop is an image editing software package that uses a file format denoted by the suffix '.PSD'. It has become so popular that it is practically a 'standard' file type and therefore extremely common. It is able to support enhanced colour information (better even than TIFFs) and holds other image edit specific information. Some non-Photoshop software packages use this file type even though it may be called something else in those programs. It creates large-sized files.

GIF Format

Another compressed format for images uses the suffix '.GIF' and was originally designed for Internet applications such as web site graphics. It uses a very limited set of colours (just 256) and is ideal for graphic images with large expanses of even colour. Photographs saved in GIF format lose a great deal of colour information and any smooth gradations between shades of the same colour. This can make the image looked 'stepped'.

RAW Format

RAW files are created in the camera without any in-camera processing affecting the data. They provide all the information captured by the camera's sensor. You can process the images later on PC and access all the unprocessed information within the image file. You will need special software to be able to edit RAW photos which is usually supplied with the camera.

PICT Format

This is a file type developed for use on Apple Macintosh computers designed primarily for on-screen only images with a limited resolution. It offers a way to see an image with very basic software, so even some text programs will be able to see a PICT file, although they cannot be used to edit it.

PNG Format

Another lossless compression format, PNG (suffix '.PNG') is built for use over the Internet and is therefore ideal for web images. It supports information on colour, greyscale and true-colour images and is designed to be a more advanced replacement for the GIF file format.

PDF Format

The Portable Document Format (suffix '.PDF') is a file type that is used by Adobe Acrobat. As its name suggests though, the document can be looked at anywhere. You need to have the Adobe Acrobat Reader software to do so, but it should be included free with your computer operating system. You cannot edit the document with 'Reader'.

PDF is ideal for use on documents such as newsletters or other designed jobs that will be printed, such as posters, because it retains information about the images, typography, graphics, text and the layout all together within the document.

WHEN TO USE EACH FORMAT

- **TIFF**: Lossless compression with best quality for images that are to be printed.

- **JPEG** or JPG: Lossy compression format, ideal where quality needs to be retained but memory space is at a premium.

- **PSD**: The generic file format used by the popular Photoshop editing programs, again for high quality usage.

- **GIF**: Lossless file format designed for web graphics. Not for printed photographs.

- **PNG**: Offers lossless compression and is ideal for Internet use, similar to 'GIF' but better quality.

- **RAW**: RAW images are composed of the raw data as captured by the camera sensor. Most, if not all, digital SLRs have this option as do many of the more advanced 'enthusiast' compact style digital cameras. Most current image editing packages can edit RAW files; alternatively use the software that comes with the camera.

- **PICT**: An Apple Macintosh specific format designed for use on on-screen images with a limited resolution.

- **PDF**: A cross platform file format readable by most computers and ideal for news letters, posters or letters containing graphics and text.

This shot has been split into three elements. The top section is a TIFF file, the central portion a high quality JPEG and the bottom third a very low quality JPEG. The enlarged area shown below reveals the blocky JPEG artefacts caused by the JPEG compression from the area indicated in the rectangle above. The high quality JPEG has almost no visible problems at all. Also, note the way the colours have blocked together in the water below the washing man.

Auto & Quick Fix

Image editing packages provide easy-to-use tools that allow you to make fast edits to images at the click of a mouse. Here's how to make the best of these 'auto' or 'quick fix' tools.

A quick fix is exactly that, a fast and easy way to adjust common problems, such as low contrast or under and overexposure in an image, simply by using a couple of clicks of your mouse. Some packages call it 'auto fix' or 'smart fix' because the program itself analyses the image, looks for problems that either make the image dull or colourless and then adjusts the settings to compensate.

Each editing package works in a similar way and, whichever software you use, the auto fix has a similar effect - improving the image. The function is usually found in a drop-down menu.

With the image you want to be fixed open in the program, highlight the auto fix option and the program will go to work. If your software has other settings such as auto levels, auto contrast and auto colour correction, each operates in the same automatic way applying corrections according to their titles. If one produces an unsatisfactory result, try one of the others. The auto fix however (as it works across all the image variables at once) will usually be sufficient for most minor image corrections.

Some packages allow you to adjust the amount of correction that is applied as you go. This is ideal if, after applying an auto fix, you think it has overdone the 'fix'.

Other programs have a preview screen that provides a before and after window (as the example below illustrates) to show how the edit will affect the image. This allows you to adjust the amount of auto fix applied by judging its effect 'live' on screen.

Fixing Colour Casts

In this shot taken indoors in a museum, the display's lighting has created an unnatural orange colour cast that has completely hidden the true colours of the statue. Using an auto fix, the program has analysed the shot and completely removed the orange colour cast, without affecting the dark background thus revealing the true, more neutral bluish colour of the statue.

Fixing Low Contrast

In images such as the top one here, where there's little contrast (contrast is simply the difference between the blackest and whitest areas in a shot), the whites are muted, the blacks look brown or grey and detail is pretty much invisible. An auto contrast fix can work wonders here. In the second shot, the auto

contrast fix has checked the image for the brightest and darkest parts, and fixed them. It has boosted the colours as well, making the shot look brighter and more natural.

Fixing Exposure Problems

Under and overexposure can be adjusted in auto fix too. Underexposure is caused when the camera has not recorded enough light to get a bright, colourful image; over-exposure is the opposite. Using auto fix will help brighten or darken an image. The cake shot shown below was underexposed, but with auto fix it has been brightened and the colour has been enhanced.

A problem with correcting exposure issues however, is that the auto fix can sometimes overdo the processing. This means you may lose detail in some areas of a shot and colours may be adversely affected. You may need to judge the amount of auto fix you apply if this is the case.

Cropping

There's no need to worry if an image isn't framed as you'd like. The cropping function of your imaging software is a great way to remove unnecessary details from a scene or to add emphasis to a shot.

Cropping an image can be done at the beginning of the photography process, when you take the snap, or later on when you edit the images on PC. The process you go through when taking a picture – zooming in for example – is a form of cropping. It simply means cutting away parts of the scene in order to improve a photo or to remove aspects you don't want. All image editing programs contain tools to crop images.

Removing Unwanted Detail

As the images on the facing page and below show, cropping can dramatically improve a photo. Just as they took the snap below, the photographer caught a disembodied arm protruding into the bottom-right of the shot. This is a very distracting intrusion indeed. Cropping, as shown in the image above right, has removed this and helps to emphasise the viewer's attention on the main 'action' in the finished photograph, below right.

Using the Crop Command

By clicking on the crop icon, the cursor changes to the cropping tool. You then click the mouse button, hold it down and drag the cursor across the image to mark out the area you want to crop around.

If you don't get it right first time, don't worry. The hatched line that will have appeared, denoting your currently selected crop area – everything outside of which is deleted – has a series of small, box-like 'handles' half way along each edge and at the corners. They can be clicked and dragged to a new position to fine-tune the crop or even rotate the cropped area.

Once you are happy with your

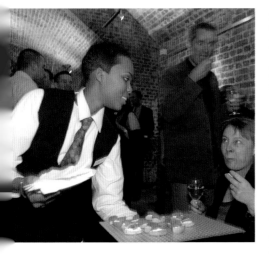

Below left: The intrusive disembodied arm.
Above: Cropping removes this distraction.
Below: The finished photograph.

selection, double click inside the crop area indicated by the hatched line and the unwanted, 'cropped away' parts of the image, indicated with a shaded area, will be deleted, completing your crop. Remember to save the image once you've finished.

Creative Cropping

Cropping can also be used to change the emphasis of a shot, alter its format or to zoom in on a smaller area of interest. This improves its creative merit. Here's an example of a shot which has been cropped to create extra emphasis on the model and her extraordinary finger nails. Removing the background also helps balance the photo.

Pixels and Memory Considerations

Cropping not only removes unwanted parts of an image but, as it is permanently deleting areas of the shot, it is also removing pixels. The number of pixels in an image directly affects the file size, so when you remove them by cropping, you also reduce the file size of the image. A 50% crop of an image will reduce the file size up to three quarters. While this saves on computer memory, it also has implications for printing as the larger the file size and the more pixels you have, the larger the print can be (see *Printing* for more details).

So always consider what you want to do with an image later if the intended crop is to be a large one. This is another reason why it is always better to shoot images at the digital camera's maximum resolution – you will always have the optimal number of pixels to play with for larger cropping edits.

Straightening

Probably the most common problem for any photo is the sloping horizon effect. Luckily, with image editing it's easy to rectify.

Sloping or lopsided images are caused when the camera is not held sufficiently level, and so can happen very easily. The safest way to avoid this is to use a tripod, and to make sure that the camera is level before you press the shutter button. However, setting up a tripod is not always practical, and often you may not even realise that your picture is not level until later when you look at the image on PC.

There's a simple image editing function which can quickly correct a sloping horizon. Straightening the horizon is particularly important in landscape images that need to be printed at larger scales, say for framing on the wall.

This straightening function does crop a little of the original image but not enough to cause major problems. Here's how to do it.

Step 1:
Open the image to be straightened and activate the 'grid' overlay pattern, in this case using the **View > Grid** command. A grid of lines and squares will overlay the image, but will not affect the image as the grid sits over the picture.

This image has an unnatural sloping horizon that needs to be straightened.

Step 2:

Using the grid of lines and squares as a guide, use the **Image > Rotate > Free Rotate Layer** command. Depending on the software, a box may appear asking you to make a 'layer'; don't worry about this but click the 'OK' button. The image is now transformed into a movable image layer called something like 'layer 0'. You'll see a new box appear around the image with handles similar to those used to crop an image.

Hover the mouse cursor over a corner handle and little arrows appear indicating you can rotate the image in either direction.

Step 3:

The technique's the same as for cropping an image: you click and hold on a corner handle but this time rotate the image until the horizon is aligned correctly with the overlaying grid.

Once you're satisfied the horizon's straight, double click inside the image and the transformation will be complete. You will see however, areas around the edge of the straightened image where cropping is required to tidy up the edge. Simply use the previous topic's crop technique to complete the image edit and then you're done. Now save your image.

The final straightened image, without the sloping horizon.

Resizing

It's very simple to change the resolution, dimensions or file size of an image. Here's how and why to resize your photos.

Whether you need to reduce the resolution and file size of an image for use with email or the Internet, or you want to enlarge the file in order to print the image at a size that its current resolution would not otherwise allow, there is a simple method to achieve your goal: the 'resize' command.

Resampling

When you resize an image you can change its output size without altering its physical, pixel or file size. Or you can 'resample' the image, which actually changes the dimensions of the pixels as the image is resized, and therefore its file size will alter too. Resampling is necessary in some circumstances, but to be avoided in others. Let's look at some examples to explain what's involved.

Making Images Smaller

Here's how to resize an image which is only needed at a small size, for use on a website for example. Resampling will reduce the file size, but won't be detrimental to the quality of the final smaller image.

Step 1:

To make an image smaller, open the image you wish to reduce in size and use the **Image > Resize > Image Size** command, which brings up a new dialogue box indicating the current size of the photo. Specifically, it presents information on the pixel dimensions, the document's size in centimetres and the current resolution, and the resample check box as shown here.

Step 2:

To reduce the resolution from 300 pixels to screen resolution, 72 pixels per inch (ppi), click the 'resample' check box and the 'constrain proportions' check box which ensures the aspect (height-to-width) ratio of the shot will not change, then type '72' into the 'resolution' box.

Notice how when you click in the resample box, the 'pixel dimensions' box becomes editable. Click OK to make the change. The image will shrink on screen to its new size. Use the **File > Save As** save command and give the new, smaller image a new name, otherwise it will overwrite the original file and you'll lose it.

Making Images Bigger

Here's how to increase the size of an image so that it can be printed at a larger size. This can be done with resampling, thus increasing the size of the file, or without resampling, leaving the file size unchanged.

If resampling, the software will use interpolation, which is the name given to a calculation that adds pixels based on those that are already there. Unfortunately, interpolation can cause a softening or blurring of your image as the program 'guesses' what pixels to add.

Step 1:
Open the image you want to enlarge and use the **Image > Resize > Image Size** command here to bring up the image size dialogue box.

As discussed, there are two strategies that can now be used to make the image bigger: with resampling, which changes the file size, or without resampling.

Step 2:
To resample and make an image bigger, check the resample and constrain proportions boxes, and type the required dimensions into the width or height boxes. Typing in one affects the other and the pixel dimensions will change as well as the file size, which will increase dramatically. To keep the quality, don't enlarge an image with the resampling set to more than double its start size.

Step 3:
Enlarging without resampling requires typing the required dimensions into the height or width boxes but leaving the resample check box clear. The file size and pixel dimensions remain unchanged, but the 'document size resolution' has now reduced. To keep print quality high,

don't let this drop below around 180ppi. Use the **File > Save As** save command resaving the shot without overwriting the original image.

Resizing Example
These three images below reveal the effect resizing with resampling has on both the pixel dimensions and the file size. The largest image has 2048x7032 pixels with a file size of 18MB, ideal for printing at over A4. The middle image has 1536x1024 pixels and a file size of 4.5MB, okay for smaller print sizes and the smallest image has just 640x427 pixels and only a 800KB file size, ideal for email.

Sharpening

If you have a soft image or a shot not quite focused, and think it's ruined, think again. Your editing software can sharpen the image quickly and easily.

Occasionally, the very digitising process involved in creating images introduces 'softness' which appears as a slight lack of focus. All digital cameras have built in settings that can process this softness away but when you add camera shake or the camera not focusing properly, the pictures can look even less sharp.

All image editing packages have functions designed to help sharpen digital images, called 'filters'. Sharpen filters have a variety of modes but one filter stands out as the best tool in the sharpening armoury, the 'unsharp mask'.

Using Unsharp Mask to Sharpen

The unsharp mask filter is generally the best to use for sharpening, as it can be finely tuned to each image. It works by increasing the contrast between adjacent pixels, the higher the contrast at these pixels, the more the unsharp mask works. Because these points usually represent an 'edge' in an image, the overall effect is to sharpen the shot.

But the settings you use will depend on the image's content; a portrait may require completely different unsharp mask settings, to say, a shot of a building. Here's an example that will make this clearer.

Step 1:
File > Open the image to be sharpened and then navigate to the unsharp tool via **Filter > Sharpen > Unsharp Mask** menus. A new dialogue box appears with a preview window and three 'sliders', which can each be dragged to a desired point.

Step 2:
The first parameter to set is the 'radius'. It controls the width around the pixels it sharpens (similar to a halo effect). Entering a radius of 1 tells the software to 'look' outwards one pixel as it evaluates each pixel. The higher the radius number, the bigger the halo of sharpening around each evaluated pixel.

Step 3:
The next setting to adjust is the 'amount'. Think of this as controlling the 'volume' for the unsharp mask as it determines the strength of the sharpening effect. A small radius setting will need a higher amount than a bigger radius setting to produce the same visual sharpening effect.

Step 4:
Last but not least comes the 'threshold' control, which acts like a noise reduction setting by instructing the software to ignore certain differences between pixels as it sharpens, helping prevent over-sharpening in areas such as skin tones in a portrait for example. Move all three sliders to get the best sharpening effect for the shot.

as it can actually be detrimental to some types of image.

Sharpen More

As you might expect from its name, this sharpen tool adds a strong focus-like effect, again better used on a smaller selection in an image rather than across the whole photo. It can improve clarity in smaller areas effectively and is a much stronger, sharper effect than sharpen.

This shot shows before (top part) and after the sharpening effect. The detail in the roof has been revealed without adversely affecting the rest of the image.

Settings For Best Results

As a rule of thumb, start by using an amount setting of 200 to 300 percent, then a threshold of zero and a radius setting to match the photos content, typically between 0.5 and 2. Overdoing the radius will generate white lines (the halos become visible) around everything with an 'edge' in the shot. You rarely if ever need a radius of more than 3 for example.

To sharpen the image above, which lacked sharpness primarily in the roof detail, the amount needed was '222', a radius of just 1 was set and a threshold of 5 used, primarily to reduce noise artefacts that appeared in the blue sky.

Other Sharpen Filters

Sharpen

The sharpen filter can be used to increase apparent focus but needs to be used sensitively. It is best applied to smaller parts of a shot rather than the entire image,

Sharpen Edges

This sharpening filter finds areas in an image where colour changes are strongest and sharpens just those points. In this way, edges can be sharpened but the overall 'smoothness' of the shot is retained. You'll find that this sharpen filter is not needed very often as unsharp mask is generally more effective.

This enlarged area shows the effect of over-sharpening an image (inside the red box). Detail around edges of pixels has been blasted and noise has been ramped up unacceptably.

Brightening & Darkening Photos

Some photos are too dark or light to be adjusted using a quick fix. But don't despair, the photo can still be rescued.

Images can come out 'too dark' or 'too light' due to under or overexposure, meaning they have detail missing in their shadow or highlight areas: the pixels have just gone completely white or completely black. These problems can be improved by putting back some of that detail to brighten or darken the problem areas. This is usually very successful for shadow areas. Highlight areas *can* also be improved but not usually to such a large degree.

Brightening an Image

Depending on your software, you'll have a menu offering a control for highlights and shadows and/or a levels adjustment control. We deal with levels, a more advanced method of adjusting lighting and colour, later in the topic *Levels*. Let's stick with the 'shadow' and 'highlight' controls here.

Step 1:
File > Open the image that needs to be lightened. In your

image editing package, choose **Enhance > Adjust Lighting > Shadow/Highlights** or equivalent from the drop-down menu.

Step 2:
Drag any of the three lighten shadows, darken highlights or midtone contrast adjustable sliders (or enter a numeric value into the relevant boxes) until you're happy with the result. In our example (below), an

This before (bottom section) and after picture shows how a 50% adjustment to the lighten shadows slider has lifted fine skin detail out of the shadowed elephant that was completely missing in the original shot.

adjustment of 50% was applied to Lighten Shadows. Ensure you check any preview box to preview the effect and accurately assess the adjustments before they're applied to the shot.

Step 3:
Click OK once you're happy, then save your photo and you're done.

Darkening an Image

Step 1:
As before, **File > Open** the image that needs editing to make it darker. In your image editing package, choose **Enhance > Adjust Lighting > Shadow/Highlights** or equivalent from the menu.

Step 2:
Drag the darken highlights and, if required, the midtone contrast sliders (or enter a numeric value into the relevant boxes) until you're happy with the result. Below a setting of 50% to the darken highlights adjustment was required and the effect on the contrast meant an additional adjustment to the midtone contrast was needed, in this case plus 10% . Once again, check the preview box to preview the effect and accurately assess the adjustments as they're applied.

Step 3:
Click OK once you're happy and then save your photo and you're done.

In this shot, the image was overexposed and as a result, all the highlight detail had gone from the clouds and colour has been leached too. Using the darken highlights and midtone contrast correction has recovered most, if not all, the detail and colour previously not visible.

Removing Redeye

We've all had pictures of our friends and family ruined by the dreaded 'redeye'. But even if your camera can't prevent it, you can still edit it out.

PREVENTING REDEYE

Redeye is caused when light from a camera flash is reflected from the back of the eye (the retina) into the lens. The closer together the camera's lens and flash, the more likely it is your photos will suffer from redeye. Redeye is red because the blood vessels in the eye colour the reflected light producing the effect you see in your photos.

It becomes most prevalent in low light when the subject's pupil is bigger and in children, whose eyes and pupils tend to be naturally bigger all the time. It's a common problem simply because of the small size of most modern digital compacts. Their tiny size means the flash and lens are always quite close together and hence the reason practically all digital cameras have a redeye reduction mode.

To help prevent or reduce the redeye effect always make sure the redeye reduction mode is on when shooting with flash and/or in low light. The redeye mode will either fire a burst of quick flashes or project a beam of light towards the subject before the shutter fires. This has the effect of helping reduce the iris's size, thus reducing the pupil size and so reducing the redeye effect in the final shot.

Redeye is a common problem with today's small digital compact cameras, which even with their redeye reduction modes (see left) can still produce shots marred by *that* demonic look.

If you have a shot with redeye don't worr most editing software packages have a simple-to-use tool for removing or reducing the effect, saving an otherwise ruined phot

This slow sync shot taken at night has a dramatic redeye problem. Let's see how we can fix it.

Step 1:

File > Open the image that needs redeye removing. Using the zoom or magnify tool, magnify the eyes of the subject suffering redeye by clicking and dragging around the eyes with the magnify tool. This will enlarge that portion of the photo sufficiently to work on.

Step 2:

Click on the 'redeye removal' tool and in the same way you clicked and dragged the image to magnify it, click and drag the redeye tool around each eye separately. The software will 'look' at the red pixels and replace them with a dark grey series of pixels (also preserving any catch lights in the eyes – as shown above) producing a natural looking pupil colour.

Step 3:

Repeat steps one and two above for each person suffering the effect in the shot until the redeye is removed.

Step 4:

Save your photo and you're done.

The same slow sync flash photo after the redeye reduction tool has been used. It has produced a natural looking effect, keeping the catch lights and rescuing an otherwise unusable picture.

Creating Black & White

You can easily create black and white photos from colour shots - ideal if you want to make a dramatic change of emphasis in an image.

Removing the colour from a perfectly good image may seem a little odd but it is a useful device when a shot has not worked the way you intended in colour. There may be distracting colours in a portrait image or the texture and shapes in the photo may strike you as something that could be better treated in black and white or 'mono'. Some images have such muted colours that it may be possible to derive more impact from a mono version than the original colour image.

Subtle Colour to Black and White

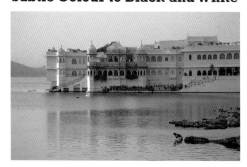

This photo of a lake in India has such subtle hues and tones that it is an ideal shot to use this technique on.

Step 1:
File > Open the image that you'd like to convert to black and white. Use the **Enhance > Adjust Colour > Remove Colour** command, or use your software's equivalent - it may be called 'desaturate'.

Once the 'remove colour' command is activated, all the colours in the original image's pixels are given equal red, green and blue (RGB) values but lightness is not changed. This actually gives you the black and white effect. But it's possible the shot can have a lack of contrast. Without definition between blacks and whites it looks almost too grey.

Step 2:
If the image does lack contrast then a quick fix (or smart fix or auto fix depending on your software) will help sort it out. Follow the steps in the topic *Auto & Quick Fix* to apply a quick fix and you'll find the image's blacks become blacker, the whites whiter and overall the contrast will be improved.

Step 3:
File > Save your image with a new name.

The finished image works well in black and white thanks to the graphic-looking nature of the subject matter.

Strong Colour to Black and White

Other types of image, such as the one below, have deep shadow and stronger contrast - features which also lend themselves to a mono treatment. Here, the dark background and lighter skin tones would be a great graphic contrast in a mono shot.

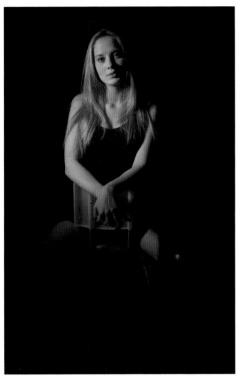

Step 1:
File > Open the image that needs converting to black and white. Use the **Enhance > Adjust Colour > Remove Colour** command as before. With the remove colour command activated, all the colours in the original image are changed to black and white once more. However, because of the dark background and lighter skin, the emphasis on the woman needs to be improved.

Step 2:
Because this image has stronger areas of contrast than the previous shot, a quick fix won't do it any good, it'll just try to equalise the dark and light areas, and ruin the shot.

This time use your software's **Enhance > Auto Colour Correction** command or equivalent. This looks at the (now grey) pixels. These all have equal RGB values, but with untouched 'lightness' parameters, so this command boosts the brightness of less grey pixels. This adds punch without damaging the blacker parts of the shot.

Step 3:
File > Save As your image and give it a new name so that you don't overwrite the original colour shot.

Colour Management

The way a colour is displayed on a PC's screen can vary dramatically when printed by an inkjet printer. Here's how to ensure the colours you see when you take a photo are the colours you get on screen and on the printed photo.

Digital cameras, computer screens and digital imaging devices, including scanners and printers, have their own specific way of 'seeing' and representing colours. These are called colour profiles, and in order to reproduce colours consistently across all of your digital devices, you'll need to ensure that they all use the same profile. This is the essence of colour management.

RGB and CMYK Colours

In the digital domain, colour is represented in two ways. The first, on a PC screen for example, uses red, green and blue (RGB) pixels which combine to create all the colours of the rainbow. The second is via coloured inks from printers that use a basic set of four colours, cyan, magenta, yellow and black, often abbreviated as CMYK. These four colours are used to represent the RGB colours, which are converted by your printer when printing your photos.

Getting Accurate Screen Colour

Helpfully, most digital cameras and devices have industry standard colour management systems built into them. However, it's important that you can see them properly on screen,

particularly when you want to manipulate colours using editing software (as we'll discuss in the following topics of this book).

So the first thing to do is to calibrate your PC's screen so that it uses the correct colour settings. This ensures it has the correct brightness and that its colour balance is set properly. The set-up process is judged by eye and is best carried out with as dark a background as possible for optimal accuracy. Consult your manual or on-screen instructions about how to do this accurately – most PCs will have a handy software wizard to guide you through the process. Once completed, you're prompted to save the information as a profile, which other programs, such as image editing software, can use to ensure colour is properly displayed.

You'll probably find that the colour accuracy of your monitor is almost spot-on out of the box. However, it is worth checking as so much of your later colour work will be based on this.

Colour Gamut

The 'colour gamut' is the name given to the range of colours available on a specific device, such as a digital camera, PC screen or inkjet printer. The larger or 'wider' the gamut, the more colours the device has at its disposal. This is usually represented by a diagram or graph which shows all of the colours visible to the eye (the total gamut) and those colours within that which are actually able to be used by the device, indicated with a triangle inside the graph's colour range - as shown here.

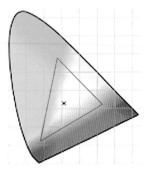

Typically, printers have a range of colours smaller than those available to your digital camera or even your PC screen. This is because greens and blues reproduce poorly on paper as do purples and oranges. However, with your screen calibrated correctly you'll be able to get a good idea of what a finished print might look like before printing and you'll be amazed at how lifelike it can look despite these apparent drawbacks.

In the set-up or preferences of all of your connected devices, such as printers or image editing software, ensure they all use the same colour settings, i.e. the same colour profile. One profile known as 'Adobe RGB' (sometimes called 'Full RGB') is particularly good because it has a larger gamut than many other image profiles, meaning it has more colours to utilise and is therefore ideal for digital images. Or use any profiles you have previously saved if you're happy with the results they produce.

Another common profile is called 'sRGB' which uses fewer colours than Adobe RGB for example and is typical of colour profiles used on the Internet and in many digital cameras.

Colour Settings in your Software

The image editing software you use will have a colour settings section that will always either preserve or convert the images you

open in it to a specified colour profile, one that ensures standard colour control across all devices.

Some digital cameras even allow you to save a specific colour profile into an image. Adobe RGB is one such profile and your camera will have a menu that allows you to embed this into your images. This is a good idea as Adobe RGB is an industry standard setting that can be used on PC too and as we've seen, has a large colour gamut.

To check the colour management in your software, go to the colour preferences or colour settings control panel and ensure the program can use Adobe (or Full) RGB. Switch on the 'full colour management' setting as shown below.

This is a typical colour set-up screen with full colour management checked ensuring all images have their colour profiles preserved or adjusted to Adobe RGB, the setting with the largest colour gamut.

COLOUR: AT A GLANCE

- Use the same colour profiles across all devices, ideally Adobe RGB (sometimes called 'full RGB'), which is the best setting for printing digital images.

- Use sRGB for images used on the Internet.

- Calibrate your monitor and always recalibrate it if you move its location or you change any ambient lighting arrangements around your workstation.

Adjusting Colours

It's easy to change and improve the colours of your images digitally.

All image editing software on the market provides for the control and adjustment of colour. Some of the more professional image editing packages will even provide you with individual controls for each element of colour. Some colour tools allow you to completely replace one colour with another, which can give dramatic effects.

For now, let's concentrate on getting the existing colour as accurately rendered as we can.

Controlling Colour Balance

Colour balance is simply the term used to describe the overall tones and hues in an image. The colour balance control can be used to make global changes to any image to help make the balance more natural, ideal for fast removal of odd colour casts.

Depending on your software, you'll have tools for controlling 'hue', 'saturation', and 'colour intensity'. Some will have a method of removing colour casts and most will have a tool which shows how variations of colour would affect your images.

Removing Colour Casts

Step 1:
File > Open the image you wish to adjust and use your software's colour adjustment tools to bring up the colour control dialogue boxes, in this case the remove colour cast dialogue box. By clicking with the 'pipette'

icon that appears on grey, completely white or completely black areas of the shot, this tool neutralises colour casts by ensuring everything black, white or grey is actually black, white or grey. Trial and error may be required to get a pleasing result.

This shot of a model with her digital camera has an odd, orange colour cast on the skin that needs to be removed to make a more flattering shot.

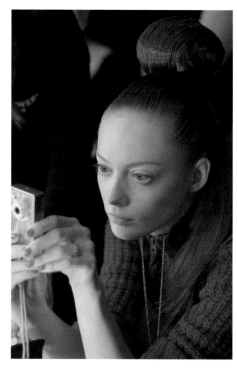

Adjusting Hue and Saturation

If the colour cast tool doesn't achieve the desired result then the next weapon to use is the adjust hue/saturation tool.

Step 1:

The Hue/Saturation tool offers a powerful suite of colour control options. A drop-down menu offers various individual colour range settings, such as reds, greens, cyans and yellows (as shown below) or a 'master' control that affects all the colours at once by moving the hue, saturation and lightness sliders.

Step 2:

The 'intensity' slider can be moved to fine-tune any effect and by clicking one of the smaller thumbnail images once the slider's been moved (each small thumbnail previews the change), the change is applied to the larger, 'after' thumbnail, as above. Specific software programs may vary a little in the layout of the controls, but the process is the same.

Step 2:

Move the hue, saturation and lightness sliders. This affects the colour range displayed in the image. Subtle movements of each slider are all that's required to remove any colour cast – or add a colour cast should you wish too.

Adjusting Using Colour Variations

To compare the effect of your changes with the original image, use the 'colour variations' tool.

Step 1:

The colour variations tool allows you to make fine adjustments to an image by selecting the brightness values you want to adjust. You have a series of buttons for midtones, shadows, highlights and saturation, depending on where you want the change to be applied in the shot. Large thumbnails of the image represent the 'before' and 'after' versions.

The finished shot with the skin tones edited back to a more normal colour. Whichever of the methods is used, the application of such colour control can make a big difference to your photos.

Levels

Want to manipulate colour but with improved control over brightness?
Use 'levels' to achieve this.

Using levels is another powerful way to control colour. It offers greater control over brightness than, say, the colour balance tool; each colour can be adjusted separately and the settings can also be saved for use on other photos in many software packages.

Levels use histograms (shown below and represented by the black curve shape within the graph) to represent the colour values in a shot. A histogram is a simplified graphic representation of the pixels in an image, graphing the colour intensity at each level, hence the name of this tool. In other words, it shows you the amount of colour in the image from the darkest pixels to the whitest and it allows you to manipulate the coloured pixels in order to improve colour rendition, brightness and contrast.

Using Levels Control

The levels control is accessed via your image editing program's **Enhance > Levels or Image > Adjustment > Levels** menus. When activated, a dialogue box presents you with a histogram display of the colour values, a drop-down menu for the colour channels and small triangle sliders; one each for black, grey and white.

The aim of the levels control is to move the triangular sliders under the histogram to align them with the graphed pixels in the display. In this way, the colour is optimised across the spread of pixels.

The 'channels' drop-down menu chooses the colour that will be adjusted while the sliders can be moved freely to make changes in each colour, the changes affecting just the colour selected. Alternatively, the global RGB channel can be selected; all three colours are edited together. Also, the two black and white sliders affect the overall darker and lighter value pixels of the colours being worked on, so adjusting image contrast.

The top-left image on the opposite page shows how the pixels in the red channel have crowded into one end of the histogram – towards the right, 'brighter' side. By moving the black slider and aligning it with the first pixels in the histogram, the red in the image deepens. Moving the white slider in the other direction would remove red from the shot.

them with the pixels in each colour channel. Note the colour changes and then tweak the sliders as needed. Only adjust the grey slider to neutralise any colour casts (or add them!) and to adjust the mid-tone colour levels – if required.

Step 4:
Once you're happy with the result (which will depend on each individual image), click OK and the changes will be applied. **File > Save** (or **Save As**) the image to finish.

Other Levels Controls

Other controls include an 'auto' button, which automatically makes adjustments for you in a similar way to a quick fix. And there are three small pipette icons, one each for black, grey and white. By selecting these pipettes and clicking in those areas in the image that are supposed to be black, grey or white, the levels control will try to make the image more neutral, making whites whiter and blacks blacker for example. This is another useful tool for removing colour casts.

Controlling Colour and Brightness

Step 1:
File > Open the image you wish to edit and using levels, the first step is to assess the histogram and check the preview tick box so that the changes you make can be seen before they're fixed into the shot.

Step 2:
Click the channels drop-down menu and select each red, green and blue colour in turn – adjust each as you go, as described above.

Step 3:
If the histogram reveals that the pixels do not reach both ends of the graph at any point, move the relevant – endmost – slider(s) to align

In this shot, the colour is muted and contrast is quite low, making the flower shot look very drab. Enter the levels control.

The finished image after adjusting the levels has boosted the natural colour – but not excessively – and sorted the contrast too.

Curves

Want fine control of the tones and brightness within your image? The 'curves' command gives you this.

Curves offer the type of control gained using levels. However, because its edits are more precisely located within the tonal reproduction of your image's brightness values, careful management of curves allows you to fine tune colour balance in your photos, without affecting any other part of the image. Let's have a look at how it works.

Using Curves

Although full of detail, which we don't want to lose, this waterfall image lacked dynamism. Using curves can bring out the best of the image without damaging the detail in the highlights of the waterfall. Here's how to do such an edit where all three red, green and blue colour channels can be adjusted together.

Step 1:

File > Open the image you wish to edit and activate curves. Notice the 'curve' is a straight, 45-degree line running from the bottom left (representing the blackest parts of the image) to the top right of the graph (the whitest parts of the shot) through the central (analogous to the grey areas) part of the graph/image. Click the preview tick box so that changes you make can be seen before they're fixed into the shot.

Step 2:

Click the channel drop down menu and select the red, green and blue colours in turn to adjust specific colours or, as with this example, leave it at the RGB (global) setting to adjust all three red, green and blue channels together.

This image of a waterfall is very subdued, lacks colour and contrast, but any adjustments need to preserve the delicate filigree of the waterfall. Levels could be used, but it might be too strong for the delicate nature of the detail in the waterfall. Using curves is the answer here.

WHAT CURVES CAN DO

Curves can be applied to all three RGB colours together or to each of these three channels in turn – depending on what you want to remove/add/adjust. You can also try the auto button and see if that takes care of any problems for you.

Altering curves separately for each of the red, green and blue channels offers an amazing amount of control over colour balance. These changes are produced so that any new colours will smoothly blend with those of the original shot.

The finished image after applying curves. The distinctive 'S' form of the curve (shown at the bottom of the page) is typical of the edit used to boost the mid-tones in a shot. In this case, where the image needed delicate colour control, a global RGB edit of the mid-tones has worked wonders without affecting the delicate detail of the waterfall.

Step 3:
Click on the line in the mid-point of the diagonal line in the graph. Note how you can click and hold the handle that appears and move it about, changing the curve as it moves. This makes changes to the image, which you can preview on screen.

Step 4:
Repeat Step 3, this time adding a handle at the mid-way point between the central handle placed in Step 3 and the top right corner. Do the same in the bottom left corner. Pull these new handles back towards the 45-degree angle, thus creating the S shape of the curve. Note how the colour and contrast have adjusted. The colours are much stronger and yet detail in the misty waterfall is retained.

Step 5:
Move each handle to achieve the best colour contrast boost for your image, and then, when you're happy, click OK to apply the changes to the shot you're editing. If you don't like an adjustment you've made you can simply click on a handle, drag it off the graph and the curve line will snap back to its starting point, ready for you to start again - a very useful feature. Try it…

Also worth remembering at this point is that if you were adjusting individual colour channels (we look more at this in the next topic *Advanced Curves*) you'd carry out similar adjustments for each of the three channels until you're happy. A 'global' RGB adjustment may not even be required in this case.

Step 6:
Don't forget to **Save** (or **File > Save As**) your image to make sure you don't lose the edits.

The curves graph after the RGB channel adjustments have been made. Note the distinctive 'S' shape of the curve. Multiple handles can be added along the line at any point for even finer control.

Advanced Curves

Whilst you can use the curves control to edit an image sensitively, it also offers more extreme creative effects.

There are some simple but radical ways to play around with your digital images using curves. From neon-glow shots to 'negative' effects, curves offers plenty of tricks. You can even draw your own curve.

Creating a Curve

Creating a custom curve by drawing it onto the graph can help make fine adjustments to specific parts of the curve or allow dramatic edits to be made. Here's how.

Step 1:
File > Open the image to be adjusted in curves and access the curves dialogue box, typically through an **Image > Adjustments > Curves** menu, depending on your software.

Step 2:
Click on the 'pencil' icon tool when the curves box appears. This will change the cursor to a

small pencil icon. Now you can draw (click and drag the pencil icon) the

The pencil icon activates the curves 'drawing' control, so you can draw any curve you desire onto the graph.

shape you desire over the 45-degree line already shown. Here (below, left) three severe spikes were added at three points along the line in the RGB channel.

Step 3:
Click the standard curves edit button to reactivate the 'normal' curves control. This will show the just-edited curve but with new handles at each peak and trough in the line. You can edit these points further if you wish or use the smooth button to reduce the aggressiveness of the curve's steep sided peaks and troughs, calming the effect.

The same curve after the pencil tool has been switched off: new handles can be pulled to continue the edit further if required. Many handles can be used to provide finer edit control along the curve.

Step 4:
Click OK and then **File > Save** (or **Save As**) to save the edits you've made.

This is the result of using curves to their extremes. 'Normal' colours can be distorted or replaced with startling colour combinations.

Negative Curve Effect

You can create a negative effect using curves too. It's great for special effects and here's the way to do it quickly and easily.

Step 1:
File > Open the image to be adjusted as in Step 1 of Creating a Curve.

Step 2:
Ensuring you're in the RGB channel, slide the topmost (right hand corner or the white) handle all the way down the right side of the dialogue box and watch how the image becomes almost completely white.

Step 3:
Slide the bottom left (the black areas) handle all the way up to the top left of the dialogue box. Now you'll see the colours reappear, but this time they'll look just like a traditional

colour negative. And that's just what it is. By moving the sliders in this way (left), you're swapping all the lighter areas for the darker ones and vice-versa.

Step 4:
Make any final edits to the handles and once you're happy with your new, reversed and surreal shot, click OK to apply the changes, then **File > Save** (or **Save As**) to keep the changes.

Single Colour Curves

Single colour curves can be adjusted to fine tune colour in a shot, or for more fun, to make dramatic special effects using bright neon-like colours that seemed not to exist in the original shot.

Step 1:
File > Open the image to be adjusted.

Step 2:
Select each of the red, green and blue channels in turn adjusting them as you see fit for the effect you require - as shown here. You may want to adjust only one colour as this would help remove a colour cast from specific areas of the image such as the

shadows for example. In this case however, all three colours are adjusted to help give the required neon-glow effect.

Step 3:
Repeat the curves channel edit for each colour until you get the required effect.

Step 4:
Click OK and then **File > Save** (or **Save As**).

In this shot, changes have been made to remove neutral shadows and highlights and replace them with colours, giving a surreal, neon-glow look to the final image.

Channels

If you want superior black and white effects, 'channels' offers fine control.

We looked at basic methods of creating black and white images earlier, but the channels control – available in professional image editing packages such as Photoshop – offers a more advanced way of creating high-quality black and white pictures and provides extra control.

Three greyscale channels, one for red, one for green and one for blue, represent colour images. Each of these channels can be accessed and extracted to create a convincing black and white image.

Let's start by looking at the channels control and what it can do.

Using Channels Controls

The first thing to do is to assess how the image looks in each channel so that you can determine which of the three colours best represents the image as a black and white shot.

Because each channel is usually displayed superimposed over the others as a colour image you'll need to set the software to display each channel as a grey toned image.

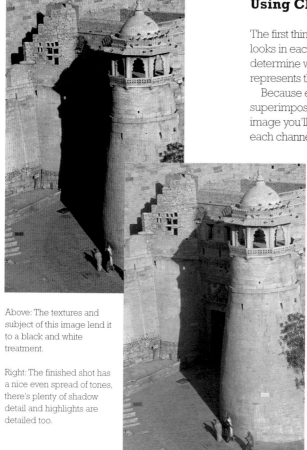

Above: The textures and subject of this image lend it to a black and white treatment.

Right: The finished shot has a nice even spread of tones, there's plenty of shadow detail and highlights are detailed too.

Step 1:
File > Open the image to be edited in channels and access the channels dialogue box; typically it is displayed to the right side of the desktop whenever an image is opened. You may have a small box with layers and paths as well as a tab for channels. Click the channels tab to make it active if it is not.

Step 2:
Small thumbnails of the open image are displayed in the channels box with a full-colour one topmost, then greyscale thumbnails for the red, green and blue channels. A small eye icon sits next to each channel thumbnail. Click the red channel's eye icon.

Step 3:

The red channel is now switched off. Notice how the image changes to a deep blue-green hue, the result of the remaining green and blue channels being left on. Click the green channel's eye icon.

Step 4:

The image should now display as a grey image, showing only the blue channel's colour information in grey tones. Double-clicking within any channel's thumbnail will display the image as a greyscale version of that colour channel. Try this and you'll soon get the hang of it.

Step 5:

Assess which of the three colour channels looks best in black and white. The red will usually be too bright, lacking fine tones and detail as there is usually a large amount of red in a photo, which looks white in its channel. Green offers a good range of greys in the shot used here (every shot could vary depending on its content) while the blue is too dark. So we have selected the green.

Step 6:

With only the green channel selected for this image, use the **Image > Mode > Greyscale** command to convert the green channel into a greyscale image. A dialogue box may appear asking you to discard the other channels. Click OK.

Step 7:

File > Save (or **Save As**) the image and now you have your black and white shot. The final image has the other colour channels removed (or extracted: this technique is sometimes called 'channel extraction') and as a result the file size will be a third smaller than the starting, full-colour shot.

THE CHANNEL MIXER

The channel mixer offers more control than that offered by simply extracting channels as it allows you to choose those colours that emphasise, say, greens over reds. In the monochrome mode, the channel mixer provides a simple way to mix all three colours as greys to control the amount of light, dark and shade to create a black and white shot.

In the full colour mode, it allows fine control of the colour too simply by adjusting each of the red, green and blue output channels. The channel mixer is reached from the **Image > Adjustments > Channel Mixer menu** and offers three sliders. Careful use of all the sliders allows you to control the hues in colour images or the way colours are mixed as shades of grey in the mono mode. To get the right look, experimentation is the key, but broadly speaking, boost greens for landscape work, and reduce blues and increase reds for shots with dramatic blue skies. Then simply tweak the slider values to get the desired results.

Below: These images show the full-colour and the three separate colour channels as greyscales when each channel is selected in the channel dialogue box. Note how the blue is very dark, the red very light but the green offers the best overall balance, making it ideal for a black and white shot.

Cloning

Stuck with unsightly blemishes or unwanted objects in a scene?
Cloning can easily remove them.

Almost everyone has taken a portrait photograph where the subject has a tree branch, telegraph pole or other odd object from the background growing from his or her head. The 'clone' tool is perfect for removing these unwanted pixels from a digital photo, by copying pixels from one part of the image and using them to cover the blemish. It can even be used to repair marked photographs by touching up scans of the damaged prints.

Using Cloning

Cloning works by creating a pixel-by-pixel copy of a part of an image, which is then applied to another area of the same image. In this case, we need to clone pixels from the sky above and around the subject to cover the pixels forming the antenna sticking out of the man's head. Of course, this could be used on any unwanted element in a shot.

Step 1:
File > Open
the image
and zoom into
the area to
be worked
upon using
the magnify

tool, leaving enough space around the part that must be cloned away to provide fresh pixels to clone over it.

Step 2:
Click on the clone tool button. The cursor will change to a small circle: effectively it has become a 'brush', which can clone pixels.

Step 3:
Pick a brush with a soft edge and size it to suit the object you're removing.

This informal portrait was taken quickly and it was not until later, reviewing the images on screen, the antenna in the distance became apparent 'growing' from the subject's head. In order to save this otherwise perfectly fine shot, cloning must be used.

Step 4:

To use the clone tool, hold the control key (or alt key on Macs) and click an area adjacent to the part of the image to be removed that has similar pixels, suitable for the background. This step selects the new pixels you'll use to cover the offending object in the shot.

Step 5:

Now click and drag the clone brush over the pixels to be removed. You'll notice the pixels from where you control/alt clicked earlier are now being copied over the pixels you want to remove.

A small cross indicates the pixel pick-up point as you progress. But, in order to ensure the pixels being cloned are as similar as possible to those being covered, frequently reselect the clone area with similar pixels to those from the background.

Step 6:

Repeat Step 5 until you've completely cloned away the offending part of the scene. The more fiddly the bit to be cloned away, the longer it will take. Zoom in closer if you need to, to get a more detailed view (you'll need a smaller brush size too). Check the 'aligned' check box to ensure the clone point is always parallel with the brush point, particularly when cloning linear subjects, as is the case in this example.

Step 7:

Once you're happy with the final result, **File > Save** (or **Save As**) the image.

The clone brush and clone pick-up cursor appear each time you click and drag over the area being cloned away. Frequent reselection of the clone point may be needed, depending on the fiddliness of the image parts that need to be removed.

Right: The finished picture now has the offending mast completely cloned away using the surrounding sky and cloud pixels to seamlessly cover it up. Practice will help you judge the best way pixels are cloned and help hone your technique.

Dodge & Burn

Want to darken or lighten small sections of an image? Here's how.

Traditional film photography darkroom techniques included 'dodging' and 'burning', where the printer of the photograph was able to allow more light into some parts of a print (the so-called 'burning in') to make them darker or hold light back ('dodging') from reaching the print, making them lighter. In essence, dodging and burning simply means you're controlling local areas of light and dark.

This has been translated to the digital domain and it is a fantastic technique to help get the tones in smaller areas just right. It can be used to brighten shadows to reveal detail in a shaded face, or to add deeper tones to, say, a landscape, where you might want to emphasise a stormy, brooding sky by deepening the tones or colours of clouds. This can all be achieved without affecting the photo as a whole.

It can be applied to black and white shots or to colour images. All that matters is that you can lift shadows if need be (dodging) or deepen them (burning). Here's how to do it.

deeper background shadows, so dodging and burning is perfect here.

Above: This shot has deep shadows in the background and on the man's face on the right. Lifting the facial shadows but darkening some of the background distractions without affecting the rest of the image will keep its contemplative atmosphere and will help direct the viewer's eye to the two subjects.

Using Dodge and Burn

The image we are working on requires two things: shadows lifted from the faces of the subjects; and a deepening of the background shadow to de-emphasise the distracting image content. We don't want to affect the whole shot, just the faces and

Step 1:
File > Open your image and select the dodge tool. Also, pick a soft-edged brush (in this case of 65 pixels) ready to start dodging.

Step 2:

Now zoom into the shadow area on which you want to work. The dodge and burn tools can be set to work on a specific range of pixels: shadows, midtones or highlights. With the dodge tool and the midtones selected, start with an exposure of around 25%, selected from the adjacent exposure menu.

Step 3:

Click and paint with the dodge tool over the shadow area you want to lighten, just a small brush stroke at a time.

Once you've zoomed in, you can work to lighten the darker areas.

DODGE AND BURN COLOUR

The process of dodging and burning colour images is essentially the same as that for black and white; lightening and darkening localised areas of an image. However, such work can sometimes make image noise more evident, so you have to be careful. Switching from midtones to shadow and highlight modes can help but experimentation is needed to see which works best on different images. But again, you need to use both dodge and burn tools sensitively or risk overdoing it. As with most image editing techniques, less is often so much more.

Step 4:

To deepen shadows, switch to the burn tool by clicking on its icon and continue to click and paint over the required pixels. The pixels being painted will begin to darken.

Step 5:

Repeat the processes of Step 3 and Step 4, going over each area, dodging shadows on faces and, as in this case, burning unwanted background detail away by deepening the shadows. Keep going until you're satisfied. You'll need to change brush sizes and the zoom ratio depending on how fiddly the task gets. The more 'zoomed' you are, the smaller the brush required and vice-versa.

Step 6:

File > Save (or **Save As**) your image once you're happy and you're done.

Below: The finished shot has lightened the man's face and deepened the background shadow to help hide distracting elements such as the plug socket on the pillar and items behind the woman's left side. The rope's been darkened too, but it's important realism is maintained. The lady's face has been dodged, brightening the eyes, as has her cowl in order to help make her stand out.

Layers

Don't risk changing your photos when image editing. Here's how to make dramatic changes without affecting your original pixels.

Layers are powerful tools available in higher-end editing packages and it's a good idea to get into the habit of always using them whenever you're image editing. While they make the edited image's file size bigger, they allow you to completely change an image. You might want to add text to a shot, add a new element from another photo, change the colours of a specific part, or add a pattern, all without affecting the rest of the image. By using layers, you can do almost any edit imaginable and yet not affect the original underlying pixels.

You can think of layers as transparent sheets of glass stacked one on top of another and onto each of which you can 'paint' images. Because the layers are transparent, you can see through them to what's below.

The bottom layer in the stack is labelled 'background', but each new layer you make can be given a name of your choice so that it is always recognisable. These layers can be worked on independently, allowing you to experiment with an effect to see if you like it. Once you've finished, the layers can be merged together to give you your finished, edited image.

Although we've not dealt with layers until now, all the image editing tasks we cover in this book can be carried out on layers.

Using this image, we'll apply a couple of easy-to-do layer edits, sorting out the colours with levels, changing the colours and then adding text.

Basic Adjustment Layer

To keep the first one simple, we'll use a simple 'levels adjustment layer' to correct colour, saturation and brightness in an image.

Step 1:
File > Open your image and navigate to the **Levels Adjustment Layer** via the **Layer > Adjustment Layer > Levels** command.

Step 2:
A levels dialogue box will appear, and a new layer icon will appear in the layers palette. The new layer is named by you and below it is the original image layer called 'background'.

Step 3:
Adjust the levels for the image in the normal way – as dealt with in *Levels*. If you click on the eye icon to close the new layer, you'll notice the image switch back to its pre-levels state. The underlying pixels have not been touched by this level's edit.

Step 4:
Once you have the levels right for the image click OK. Now you can merge the layers if required. Use the **Layers > Merge Layers** command. Notice in the layers palette how the two layers become one, simply called 'background' again.

Step 5:
File > Save (or **Save As**) your image.

Fundamental Changes

This time using layers, we'll make a more dramatic change and completely alter the colour of the sky.

Step 1:
File > Open your image and just as in Step 1 of the basic adjustment layer, adjust the levels for the image on an adjustment layer first. Once done, merge the result to give a new, correctly adjusted background layer.

Step 2:
Create another new layer, this time an exact copy of the original via the **Layer > Duplicate Layer** command. A dialogue box will appear asking you to name the new layer 'background copy'. Click OK. You now have a duplicate of the original image (after the adjustment layer has been applied) above it in the layers palette.

Step 3:
Use the **Enhance > Adjust Colour > Replace Colour** menu to bring up the replace colour dialogue box. Using the colour selection tool, click on the sky in the image to select that colour (blue here). If necessary, switch to the 'add to selection' tool and keep adding to the sky selection. If you pick too much, use the 'remove from selection' tool.

The replace colour dialogue box has selection tools (the three pipettes at the top) and a large black and white preview to help you check your selections.

Step 4:

Using the replacement section of the replace colour dialogue box, click in the result box. A new colour selection window appears. Pick any colour you like. In our case, it was bright green! Watch the sky change to the colour you selected. Once you're happy with the effect, click the OK button. Note that the change has only been applied to the new background copy layer. Clicking the icon for the background copy layer you'll see the newly changed sky colour vanish as the layer is turned off.

The bottom section of the replace colour dialogue box houses the replacement colour selection tools. Using the hue, saturation and lightness sliders you can fine-tune the colours selected.

Step 5:

If you're happy, you can either **File > Save** (or **Save As**) the image with the layers intact or merge the layers using the **Layers > Merge Layers** command and then **File > Save** (or **Save As**), permanently embedding the new coloured sky into the image.

The finished image with the sky colour replaced, but on an editable layer which means the underlying original image pixels are untouched by this extreme effect.

Adding Text With Layers

On some images, say for a home-made birthday card, you might want to add text and with layers, you can do it quickly without damaging the original pixels.

Step 1:

As before **File > Open** the image onto which you will add text (we've used the same shot here). Go through the levels adjustment on a layer again and **Layer > Merge Layer** it with the background layer if you want to embed the levels changes into the photo.

Step 2:

Use the **Layer > New Layer** command to create a new layer, this time name it 'text layer'.

Step 3:

Click on the 'horizontal type tool'. Select a reasonably large type size (depending on your image) and a typeface from the selection offered (in this case a typeface of Helvetica at 50 point size and medium bold was used).

Step 4:

Now type 'Happy Birthday' (or whatever you want to type) onto the 'text layer'. Once typed, you can alter the typeface and size by first highlighting the text and selecting any new parameters. If you want to move the text about, click on the move tool and then click on the text. By clicking and dragging it about, you can change its position as required.

Step 5:

To give it impact, select the warp text tool and select a style ('arch' in this case, below). The text will change shape – to the shape chosen – and now, using the move tool, once again position it as required.

Step 6:

Either **File > Save** (or **Save As**) to preserve the layers for future editing, or **Layer > Merge Layers** the document to create a single background layer and then **File > Save** (or **Save As**) as required.

The finished image with the text applied and distorted into an arch. This shot might not make a great birthday card but with practice, these techniques can be used to great creative effect.

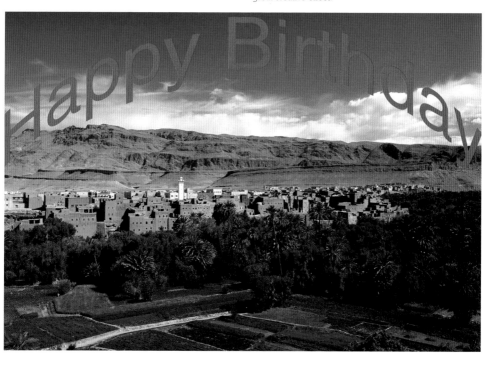

Masks

Want to protect sections of your image, whilst radically editing others?
Masking areas will keep them unaffected by any changes you make.

You can use masks to paint on effects to selected areas or paint away unwanted parts of an image. Using masks on a layer means you can use an edit or effect that does not permanently affect any underlying pixels.

Using Masks

If you want to change a large element in a photo, such as replacing the sky in one shot with pixels from another, masks come into their own. You can cover over and reveal portions of two images so that you create a composite of the two shots.

The shot of the mosque below has a bland, neutral sky so we want to add more colour; ideally matching the blue of the woman's clothing. You can use any two shots to do this, but the more simple the sky and foreground outlines on the second shot, the easier it will be.

Step 1:
File > Open both the images you're going to use, call one the 'sky' image, and the other the 'ground' image. If you haven't already done so, and they need it, apply a levels adjustment layer to both shots (as described in *Layers*) and merge the images.

The two images side by side ready for compositing.

Step 2:
Create a copy of the ground image (called the 'background' layer) in the layers palette with the **Layer > New Layer Via Copy** command ('background copy' layer may also be called 'layer 1' - depending on the software you use).

Step 3:
Using the magic wand tool (used to select all pixels of a similar colour with a single click – it looks just like a small wand), click on

the sky in layer 1. The layer will highlight to show it's the active layer. This will select the sky pixels, which must be deleted in order for the image pixels from the desired sky shot eventually to show through. Select the paintbrush tool (mask mode) and the non-sky area will change to a red mask protecting it.

Step 4:
Feather the selected sky area by about 2 pixels with the **Select > Feather** command. Feathering helps smooth hard edges, blurring them slightly to limit abrupt joins of different pixels, and making a more natural-looking fit.

Step 5:
If any of your selected sky in the ground image has not been properly selected using the magic wand tool, click on the brush tool. Check you're in selection mode and paint more selection into the area NOT already selected by the magic wand tool, in this case, the window in the wall. This new selection area will also become part of the mask. Paint more selection into the areas which need it – with an appropriate brush size and zooming as required. Remember, if you make a

mistake and paint in too much selection, switch back to mask mode and paint back in the mask again. Keep going until you're happy.

Step 6:
Hit delete to remove the sky (and other selected areas) from the ground image.

Step 7:
Select the sky image and using the rectangular marquee tool, click and drag across the entire image to select its pixels. Use the **Edit > Copy** command to copy the selected sky image. Close the sky image.

Step 8:
Click on the ground image and then click the background layer, in the layers palette. Using the **Edit > Paste** command, apply the copied sky image pixels over the ground image. A new 'layer 2' is automatically created containing the copied sky pixels, overlaying the ground image. You can check this in the layers palette. The new sky is now composed with the transparent layer 1 and you have added your new sky.

Step 9:
Click on the relevant layer if any aspect of the image requires further fine-tuning. The finished image should have three layers: a 'background', then 'layer 2' (containing the sky image) and on top, the 'masked layer 1'. Its mask/selection protects and covers the unwanted parts of the sky image. Note the bottom 'background' is untouched. Once

you're satisfied, use the **Layer > Merge Layers** command and **File > Save** (or **Save As**) your new image.

The final image will have a single background layer after merging and will have the new colourful sky pixels in place of the old, bland sky pixels. With practice, you'll be able to use this technique with multiple layers to edit in – or out – almost anything in a shot and without permanently changing the original image's pixels.

Painting Onto Layers

Another technique to use for a more creative or arty effect is to paint a mask onto a layer to protect one part of an image from a filter effect for example. Here's how to do it.

Step 1:
File > Open your image and do the levels tasks again if you need to and then, using the **Layer > Layer Via Copy** command, create a new copy layer as we did in the first task above. It will be called 'layer 1'.

Step 2:
Now use the **Layer > New Layer** command to make another layer (name it 'paint' layer in the dialogue box that appears) and make sure you have the mask mode and a soft edge paintbrush selected from the paintbrush selection drop-down menu.

Step 3:
Paint shapes over the image on layer 1 (simple squiggly lines over the food were added – below) and a red mask will be painted on, representing protected areas of the image – those that will NOT be affected by future edits. (You can also invert the mask in the **Select > Inverse** command, which means the areas not painted over will be masked and protected instead.)

Step 4:

Once you've painted your mask onto the paint layer, click on layer 1 (the background copy) to make it active and use the **Filter > Distort > Ripple** command to apply the filter (you can use any filter you wish though). Then, apply the **Filter > Sketch > Chalk & Charcoal** filter (or any other filter of your choice that's suitable for your image) to strip the colour away and add another texture effect. Note how your painted mask area has been left untouched as below.

Step 5:

Once you're happy with the effect, you need to de-select the mask/selection layer by clicking on any other selection tool (such as the rectangular marquee tool) and clicking inside the image. Then use the **Layer > Merge Visible** command to merge the layers, then **File Save** (or **Save As**).

The final effect leaves colour in the protected masked areas and the effects of the filters you've applied everywhere else.

MASKING TIPS

- **Feathering**: Feathering allows you to soften edges (it makes them fuzzy-looking) for a more realistic joining effect. You can define the number of pixels around the selection that will be feathered: the larger the number, the more pixels outward from the selection that will be made fuzzier.

- **Selections & Masks**: Selections are the area you've defined in a layer using a selection tool such as the magic wand or selection brush. You can add to a selection by painting onto the layer in mask mode. By switching back and forth, you can…

- **Add and Subtract a Mask**: If you paint too much of a selection onto a layer in selection mode, you can remove it by switching to mask mode and painting it back in again. Careful use of the right brush size and zooming allows very accurate masks to be made, even around complex features such as tree branches and hair.

Blurring Backgrounds

This pro technique allows you to emphasise your subject by reducing the impact of the background.

Adding 'blur' to a shot allows you to lessen the impact of a distracting background. This is similar to the effect of a shallow depth of field. For example, in the shot below, we want to reduce the detail in the background (the sun shade, table and chairs), creating emphasis on the person in the foreground.

Step 1:
File > Open the image to be worked upon, perform a 'quick fix/auto levels' if required and then create a duplicate layer: **Layer > Duplicate Layer** and rename it something you'll remember. Working on this layer protects the original pixels while you're editing.

This is an otherwise good image that would benefit from emphasising the figure in the foreground.

Step 2:
Working on the newly created layer, select the selection brush and in mask mode, paint a red mask around the subject which should look something like this.

Step 3:
Choose a 'soft' brush with a size small enough to paint more mask carefully around the subject, right up to the edges. This additional step means that the initial selection does not have to be very accurate - you can adjust it as necessary.

Step 4:
If you make a mistake while painting, switch back to selection mode and you'll see the selection's 'wriggly' line denoting the selected area. Paint the selection away from any overlaps on the main subject if needed. Adjust the

- Remember to feather the selections to make the edges blend more naturally with the background.

- Adding to or removing elements from selections can be achieved easily with masks.

- Step the level of blur. More blur should be applied to the parts of a scene in the distance than those close to the main subject.

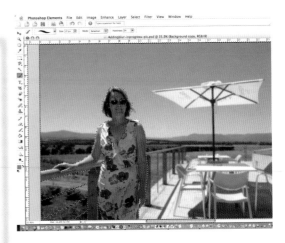

brush size to that required as you progress and ensure that the mask does not cover anything in the foreground or in front of your subject. In this case, we made sure that the fence cables and the post, level with the person, were also masked to help make the effect more natural.

Step 5:
Use the **Select > Feather** command and feather the selection by around 2 in the dialogue box that appears. This helps blend the edges of the selection making it look natural. Now, invert your selection using **Select > Inverse**. This selects the background (rather than the main subject you've been painting round with the mask).

Step 6:
Now, apply the blur effect (mimicking a large aperture lens) using the **Filter > Blur > Gaussian Blur** command. Select a level between 3 and 5, judging the effect in the preview. You can experiment to see what seems most natural. You'll notice everything except the masked subject (above, right) is now blurred. Click OK.

Step 7:
If the blur has invaded the main subject, which is not supposed to be blurred, use the **Select > Modify > Contract** command and select 1 pixel in the dialogue box that appears. This will pull the blur back very slightly (by 1 pixel) from the selected area.

Step 8:
Once you're happy with the final effect, you can flatten the layers (**Layer > Merge Layers** or **Flatten Image**) and **File > Save** (or **Save As**).

The finished image with emphasis placed on the person in the foreground by blurring the background.

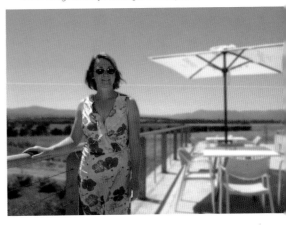

Adding Movement

This Masterclass shows how to add the appearance of movement to a photograph.

Occasionally a photo can be improved by adding 'artistic' blur, for example adding motion blur to emphasise the feeling of speed in an event.

This shot of a dancer has some natural blur in the background but to make it even more dynamic, 'motion blur' is going to be added to the main figure in the foreground. This technique can be used on multiple elements in a shot if you repeat the following process for each element.

Step 1:

File > Open the image you'll be adding motion blur to, and create a duplicate layer **Layer > Duplicate Layer**. Rename it something you'll remember and, working on this layer, apply 'quick fix/levels' if your image requires it. (From now on, let's assume that you'll already have done this where necessary on each image.)

Step 2:

We need to place each part of the scene that will have motion added onto a separate layer. Use the rectangular marquee tool to draw a rectangular selection around the subject(s) to have motion added.

Step 3:

Switch to the magic wand tool; press the alt (option) key, which allows you to remove from the rectangular selection you've already made. Keep alt (option) clicking until the selection is right. If you have a fiddly selection to make that the magic wand cannot help with, you'll need to use a mask to add to the selection. Select the selection brush in the tools palette and switch to mask mode and paint in more mask, as needed. Switch back to selection mode once you're done.

Step 4:

Now choose **Layer > New > Layer Via Cut**, which will become the 'blur layer'. Go through steps two, three and four for each element of your original image (the background layer) that you want to apply blur to. Each will become a separate layer.

Note, your background layer will have a 'hole' where each element of the image has been selected and put onto a new layer.

Step 5:

Before we add the motion blur we must use the clone tool to fill in any holes in the background layer that were left by selecting the elements for the addition of blur. Click on the background layer to make it active, use the **Layer > New > Layer** (name it something memorable, such as 'fill in holes' layer) and click OK. Select the clone tool and check the 'use all layers' check box at the top of the work area in the options bar.

Step 6:

Turn off the blur layer, and using the clone tool click in the new 'fill holes' layer. Alt (option) click on the background areas (not the holes!) and using the selected pixels, paint in the holes. With the 'use all layers' control active, it will copy pixels from the background layer to the new layer and fill in the holes. Make frequent 'alt clicks' in different areas to make sure you don't get any repeat marks from the cloning process. Keep going until the holes are filled in and to check this, make all the layers active and ensure you're happy.

Step 7:

Click on the blur layer (or each layer in turn if you have more than one) to which you'll add blur and choose **Filter > Blur > Motion Blur**. In the dialogue box select an angle for the blur that more or less follows the direction your subject's facing, and a 'distance' for the pixel blur, in this case of 27 degrees and 100 pixels respectively.

Step 8:

Once you're happy, click OK, **Layer > Merge Layers** and finally **File > Save** (or **Save As**).

The finished image, with motion blur applied has a more dynamic look giving more life to the main subject of the photograph.

Making Panoramas

Separate images can be stitched together to create a seamless panoramic image

Most image editing programs have special panorama-making tools that automate the process of joining photos together. It's relatively easy to get a good result providing you take a little care when shooting the images in the first place. You need to shoot images from the same position (ideally from a tripod), with the same focal length and with careful attention paid to the exposure values, so that the brightness is as even as possible throughout. Then you can use software techniques to remove any minor differences.

Step 1:
Use the **File > Automation Tools > Photomerge** command to launch the photomerge system. Your package may have a different name for this function, but the process is essentially the same for all software packages. A dialogue box appears asking you to browse to find your images.

Navigate to them and highlight those that will be used for the panorama. Click OK and they'll import into the software.

Step 2:
The software either automatically starts to build the panoramic image by placing the images next to each other where they overlap, or you can move them around manually into the correct order. Then it attempts to 'stitch' them together. Once completed (the length of time it takes depends on the number and size of the images being merged), the images will appear together in the window making a long, thin image. If the software (or you) make any mistakes, you can move them using the move tool. Adjust the images that require it, until you're happy with the alignment.

The finished image, consisting of separate images stitched together to create a long panoramic image.

- Always name your images something that will let you know where they should go, particularly if they're very similar shots. Left, Middle Left, Middle, Middle Right and Right for example.

- Leave image edits such as colour, brightness (levels and/or quick fixes) until after you've merged the shots. The automatic software will almost always apply an exposure correction during its processing anyway and it's best to add such edits to all the images to get a smooth and seamless look to the shot.

Step 3:
Some elements may still not fit perfectly, but don't worry, we can sort those out later. Click the 'advanced blending' check box and preview the result. You'll see where any poor exposure areas are corrected.

Step 4:
Once the merge process is complete, zoom into the image and check the merge areas have done so properly. If not, use a combination of the clone tool and the healing brush to repair any small elements of the panorama that don't quite fit, typically across the skyline. Use the healing brush for any areas without defined joins such as in the sky around clouds for example.

Step 5:
Once you're happy with the fit, you must use the crop tool to remove any uneven edges round the panorama as shown below. Try to keep as much of the image as you can. Once you're happy with the crop, double click within the crop area to crop away the unwanted panoramic elements.

Step 6:
Use the **Layer > Flatten** command to remove unwanted layers and then the **Layer > New Adjustment Layer > Levels** command and carry out general levels or auto levels (just like a quick fix) on the image to help even out any other exposure and colour problems. Once you're finished use **Layer > Merge Layers** (or **Layer > Flatten Layers**) to get rid of the unwanted layers.

Step 7:
Once you're happy, **File > Save** (or **Save As**).

Restoring Old Prints

Precious old photos don't need to be lost to dirt or scratches – you can repair them with some basic software techniques.

Scanning and editing techniques make it easy to restore damaged, scratched or dirty photographs. First off, you need to scan the original to bring it into your PC in a digital format (see *Scanning Your Photos*).The image can then be manipulated just like any of your digital photographs.

This old scanned negative below suffers from the ravages of time: it is covered in scratches and specks of dust.

Step 1:
File > Open the image, create a duplicate layer with the **Layer > Duplicate Layer** command and rename it something you'll remember. Do a quick fix/auto levels but only if your image requires it.

Step 2:
Apply a dust removal filter using the **Filter > Noise > Dust & Scratches** command but be careful as this can reduce sharpness. Use it to remove only small defects. Check the effect, monitoring changes to the radius and threshold parameters – or adjust the sliders – checking the results as you go. When happy, click OK.

Step 3:
With the topmost layer active in the layers palette, create a new layer with the **Layer > New Layer** command and rename the layer to something you'll remember, here

'clone/heal layer'. Note that this layer sits atop the first 'dust and scratches layer' and the original image (or 'background') layer.

Step 4:

Select the clone tool from the tools palette, ensuring you sample from all layers (i.e. the 'use all layers' box is checked). Magnify an area to work on and select a soft brush size from the brush menu. Make sure any brush you use is suitable for, or just slightly larger than, the dust marks you're going to remove.

Step 5:

Sample the pixels you want to clone by placing the curser over a clean area close to a mark you wish to remove. Hold down the option (or alt on a Mac keyboard) key and click with the mouse. Release the option (alt) key and click on the dust mark.Cloned pixels from the area you selected will be painted over the top of the mark.

Step 6:

Repeat this process to repair all the blemishes on the image, but remember to sample pixels from fresh areas near to the marks you want to remove. Keep going and continue to paint until the image has been cleaned up. This can take some time depending on the state of your images. Any mistakes made while cloning can be undone quickly with **Control > Z** (or **Apple > Z** on Macs).

Step 7:

Once you've finished cloning/healing and you're happy with the finished and repaired effect, you should flatten the layers (**Layer > Flatten Image**) and save your image **File > Save** (or **Save As**).

- Use the clone tool to sample pixels from one part of the image and place (or 'clone') them elsewhere.

- Repeated sampling will be required and remember to sample from similar areas to help ensure the cloned effect looks natural.

The finished, cleaned image. All blemishes have been diminished or removed, enough for a respectable-size print to be made with ease.

- Don't heal near edges

Special Effects

You can create new and unusual images
using image editing techniques.

By bringing together the image editing
techniques described in this book so far, it's
possible to completely re-invent an image.
These techniques can be used on almost
any image or element within an image to
add something to a shot. We'll work through
one fun example to demonstrate what can
be done.

This image is ideal for fun experimentation. Here we'll
swap all three heads around using layers and some
fine-tuning with the clone tool, masks and selections.

Step 1:

Open the image you want to experiment with
and create a copy of the 'background' layer.
Call it something you'll remember easily as
we'll have quite a few layers open in this
technique. This new layer will have the
background removed to help isolate the
heads or objects you're moving. Use the
magic wand tool and click on the
background to select it. Switch to the
selection brush, then add or subtract from
the background by changing between the

mask and selection modes. Paint them in until you're happy the background is selected. Change to the selection mode and hit delete to remove the background; it should look something like the image below.

Step 2:
Copy the layer from which you just removed the background with **Layer > New > Layer Via Copy** and repeat this step for each element you want to move. In this image we will use one layer for each head. Name the layers something you'll remember, in this case 'right', 'left' and 'middle head' as shown below. Turn the background layer off by clicking its eye icon in the layers palette.

Step 3:
Click on the first 'head' layer to work on and zoom in to make it easier. Using the selection brush (in mask mode) paint a selection over the element you'll be moving. Switch between the selection and mask modes to get the mask just right. Once you have it, it'll look similar to this.

Step 4:
Make sure you're in selection mode and hit delete to remove everything but the head. Repeat this on each layer in turn (if there's more than one element you're moving) and you'll be left with something like the image below. Make the background active again and use the clone tool to tidy up stray background elements (hair, ears showing through etc). Make sure you select 'use all layers' - this way you'll pick up layers from the background and paste them onto your active layer.

Step 5:
With the background still active (click on relevant thumbnails in the layers palette), select the move tool and click on the object (or head in this case) and drag it to its new location. An elastic 'box' will appear round the object you're moving, and this will have handles which can be pulled. Use the handles to rotate and change the size of the object until you're happy with the placement. Repeat this for each head/object: activate the object's layer, use the move tool to drag it into position and resize/move until it fits properly.

The only head that needed major work was the woman's. It had to be scaled up slightly using the box's handles to make it fit successfully over the man's head. The clone tool was used to tidy up the join and make the fit more convincing.

Step 6:

Once you have positioned all the objects correctly, tidy up with the clone tool and the healing brush. If needed, use the paint brush. Change each respective layer's blend mode, then use 'multiply' to darken and lighten any areas by carefully painting over them. Use the pipette tool to sample skin colour (by clicking where you want to grab colour from on the image) and then paint over a layer that requires pixels of the same colour - the paint brush will use the sampled colours. The neck of the man on the right and the woman were too light and were darkened in this way.

Step 7:

Once you're happy, **Layer > Merge Visible** (or **Flatten**) the image to remove the layers and blend everything together and then **File > Save** (or **Save As**) and you're done.

The finished image with the heads swapped around. Astute use of the clone tool and paint brush has helped blend everything nicely for a convincing swap!

Special Effects Using Filters

There is an amazing array of special effects filters, which can quickly and simply apply striking effects to your shots.

Image editing packages come with a host of special effects built in, called 'filters'. Some filters perform edit-style changes (sharpening for example), while others create special looks such as mimicking a style of art.

Each filter is applied to an image using the same steps. Filters can be used in combination with each other, and with other techniques.

Using Filters

Usually the filters are found within the filters menu for your software and are applied by scrolling the drop-down menu of filters which appears and highlighting the filter of your choice. Some filters have preview windows and sliders to adjust the values and strength of the effect before it is applied to the shot. In this way, you can quickly see if you like what the filter does before applying it to the image. Good practice when adding filter effects is to apply filters to layers so you can apply the filter effect without it changing the original pixels.

Step 1:
Open the image you want to play with and create a new layer with the **Layer > New Layer Via Copy** command.

Step 2:
Use the **Filter > Pixelate > Crystallise** (or whichever filter type you want from the menu) to activate the filter. This brings up a

dialogue box in which you select the parameters you want and then click OK.

Step 3:
Check the effect and then continue with other edits, or if you're finished, **Layer > Flatten Layers** (or **Merge Visible**) the image and **File > Save** (or **Save As**) and you're done.

Here, a combination of filters has been used with adjustment layers to alter the saturation and mask out certain layers. It shows how you can build filter effects one on top of the other.

The Lens Flare Filter

The lens flare filter produces the same effect as direct sunlight entering the lens, for various lens focal lengths. Use this effect sparingly as it can be easily overdone.

The lens flare filter dialogue box allows you to choose between lens types (50-300mm zoom in this case) and the position and intensity of the 'Sun'.

The Crystallise Filter

The crystallise filter provides a faceted effect useful for textures and making unusual shapes from blocks of colour.

The crystallise filter's dialogue box allows the adjustment of the intensity of the effect, prior to application on the image.

The Stained Glass Filter

Like crystallise, this filter applies a texture and light effect but here it is one that mimics stained glass windows.

The dialogue box provides adjustment for the size of the glass cells, the borders and the light intensity.

The Wind Filter

This filter replicates the effect that wind would have on pixels if it could blow them around on the PC's screen. Here, the wind filter was set to 'blast' and a direction of right to left chosen.

The wind filter adds streaks of pixels with the direction and intensity of the 'wind' controlled in the simple dialogue box shown here.

Using Filters With Layer Modes

Each layer you create, whatever its purpose (adding a filter, text or some other edit) can have a variety of settings applied to it. These so-called 'layer modes' can be used to make a layer more transparent or darker. They can apply special colour effects, changes to saturation or lighting styles (such as hard light or soft light) and even the luminosity can be tweaked. In short, you can adjust not only the pixels on the layer, but the way the layer behaves as well. Experimentation is useful here to help discover what each layer mode does.

This image is made up of several layers that have been manipulated both in terms of the filter effect and the layer mode control.

Layers can be adjusted to be more transparent and the type of effect the layer produces can be changed too. The fibres filter was applied to a layer at 50% opacity and then a colour burn filter was applied to boost the saturation in the areas where the fibres filter was still visible.

Making Art: Poster Effects

With this Masterclass technique, it's easy to create a perfect pop art poster from any of your images.

The starting image can be any portrait but ideally one with lots of contrast. As this image does not have that much contrast, we'll need to adjust this first and then proceed with the rest of the process.

Editing software can be used very effectively to give a portrait image a poster look. Here we'll create an example in the style made famous by Andy Warhol to show how easy it is to add a new spin to the 'traditional' portrait.

Step 1:
File > Open the image and using the **Layer > New Adjustment Layer > Levels** feature click and drag the black point and white point sliders towards the centre of the histogram. Brighten the image if needed by sliding the central (grey point) triangle towards the black point slider. **Layer > Flatten** the image.

Step 2:

Next, just like Warhol's technique, we must reduce the number of colours in the image to give us those big blocks of colour. To do this, use the software's 'posterise' feature. Create a new layer (**Layer > New Layer Via Copy**) and use the **Filter > Adjust > Posterise** command. Call it 'posterise layer' or something memorable. In the dialogue box that appears, the smaller the number chosen, the fewer the colours that will remain in the final image. Use four levels of colour as below (or whatever best fits your image). Assess this by checking the effect of your changes in the preview box.

Step 3:

Now we must increase the canvas size. Think of your image as being stuck onto a canvas the same size as the image. We must increase this canvas size in order to fit more than one image on to it. Use the **Image > Resize > Canvas Size** command and double the width and length ensuring the 'anchor point' is central, as shown below. Click OK.

Step 4:

With the posterise layer active, use the **Layer > New Layer Via Copy** four times to produce four versions of the same image. Name each one and turn the background layer off. Using the move tool, click on each layer and position its image within the new, larger canvas. Make sure there are no gaps between the four images. Use the crop tool to trim the image if necessary.

Step 5:

Now you can make the colour adjustments to each layer. Use the **Enhance > Adjust Colour > Adjust Hue/Saturation** command and create a unique colour combination for each layer using the hue and saturation sliders in the dialogue box. Click on the layer you want to work on to make it active and keep adjusting, experimenting as much as you like with each layer until you're happy with the results. Use the levels control to brighten (or darken) the layers as necessary.

Step 6:

If you're happy with the results, all that remains is to **Layer > Merge Visible** (or **Flatten**) the image and then **File > Save** (or **Save As**).

The finished image has all four layers merged into one and each image has its own colour palette, creating a bright, colourful 'Warhol-style' poster.

Making Art: Painted Effects

Turning a digital image into a 'painting' can give it a new lease of life.

With astute use of filters and masks, it's possible to create vivid digital imitations of painting styles, ideal for hanging on the wall or as unique-looking presents. In this example we'll create a look similar to the painting effect used by Impressionist artists such as Claude Monet.

This is a nice image but it lacks punch. It is therefore ideal as the basis for an art-style edit. It needs a crop to focus on the house but apart from that, we can get started.

Step 1:

File > Open the image and using **Layer > New >Layer Via Copy** create a new layer upon which we'll apply the first edits. Call it 'watercolour' and then change its blending mode to luminosity. Crop the image if necessary to close in on the detail. A slight crop was applied here to make the house larger in the frame.

Step 2:

Use the **Filter > Artistic > Watercolour** command and select levels of 8, 0 and 2 in the brush detail, shadow intensity and texture sliders respectively. Click OK to apply the edits.

Step 3:

To duplicate the background layer, ready for a new effect, click on it to make it active in the layers palette and use the **Layer > Duplicate Layer** command. You'll get a new background copy layer. Click OK. Using the layers palette options at the top, set the opacity to 50% (making the layer more transparent) and set the blend mode to 'lighten'. Move this layer (by clicking, holding and dragging it) to the top of the stack of layers in the layers palette. You'll see the darkest parts of the previous watercolour effects brighten.

Step 4:

With the new 'background copy layer' active, use the **Filter > Artistic > Fresco** command. Set the parameters to 1, 8 and 1 in the respective brush size, brush detail and texture boxes (or use the sliders to suit your image).

Step 5:

Now use **Layer > Flatten Image** to remove the layers. Then draw a selection using the rectangular marquee tool and switch to mask mode. A red mask border will appear. Select a large (200 pixels should do it) textured brush and paint around the border as shown below.

Step 6:

Switch back to selection mode, and use **Select > Feather** to a level of 2 or 3, and click OK. Now use **Select > Inverse** and hit delete, making a nice soft edge, and deselect the selection by clicking anywhere inside the image with the rectangular marquee tool active.

Step 7:

Now use **Layer > New > Layer Via Copy** and with the rectangular marquee tool, make a selection around the whole image. Switch to the selection brush and then mask mode. **Use Filter > Artistic > Rough Pastels** in canvas mode and click OK.

Step 8:

Use a levels layer to brighten things a bit more if needed, and then use the **Layer > Flatten** (or **Merge**) command to make one final layer. Finally, **File > Save** (or **Save As**) your image.

The finished image, with the artistic brushes and layer effects building together to form an impressionist-style image with a softened, border.

Output

In this section, you'll find all you need to know about how and where to output your pictures, including:

 Printing – how to get the best results

 On-line – email or build a website of your pictures

 Backing-up – send your files to secure storage

 Slide shows – display a picture collection on-screen or on TV

 Scanning – output your old prints into the digital realm

 Making money – with an on-line or traditional portfolio

Backing-Up

If you keep all your images on your PC, one computer problem could wipe out your entire picture collection. Here's how to keep it safe.

Saving your images onto additional storage that is not your main PC should be an automatic task. This is sometimes called archiving. You need to consider all your data as vulnerable and you must back-up regularly.

There are software packages available, often bundled with external hard discs or with your computer's operating system, which allow you to quickly and simply set up automatic back-up routines. This means the computer does the hard work.

This is a typical back-up window. It shows when, where and what are selected for backing-up. Some files are designated for daily back-ups while others will be backed-up on a weekly or monthly basis. You can check the status of back-ups by checking the back-up logs, ensuring everything is saved properly.

Built-in Back-Up

The most important thing, when using any back-up strategy, is to keep all your files in order on your PC. Make sure you save things logically and you know where all your files (such as your images) are on the hard disc (sometimes called the 'hard drive'). Operating systems (OS) that come with a back-up program include Microsoft's Windows XP Home Edition - likely, the single, most prevalent OS available today. But the back-up utility in XP's Home Edition (XP HE) needs installing from the discs supplied with the computer.

Here's how to activate it. Before you start, you'll need to have somewhere to save the backed-up data, such as another hard disc or a CD/DVD burner (see *Computer Accessories* and *Extra Storage*).

Windows XP Home Edition Back-Up

You may need to do some searching to find XP HE's back-up program.

Step 1:
Insert your Windows XP CD into the drive and, if necessary, double-click the CD icon in 'My Computer'.

Step 2:
On the Welcome to Microsoft Windows XP screen, click 'perform additional tasks'.

Step 3:
Click 'Browse this CD'.

Step 4:
In Windows Explorer, double-click the 'ValueAdd' folder, then 'Msft', and then 'Ntbackup'.

Step 5:
Double-click 'Ntbackup.mst' to install the back-up utility.

The Back-Up Process

While this is the process for Windows XP HE, the overall procedure is very similar regardless of the software you use.

Step 1:
By default, XP's back-up utility uses a 'wizard', making the process straightforward. Click start, navigate to 'All Programs', then accessories, then to system tools, and then click back-up to start the back-up wizard.

BACK-UP HINTS

- Back-ups should be performed on a regular basis. The frequency depends upon the maximum acceptable (to you) amount of work that would be lost in the event of a catastrophe!

- Various simple back-up software packages can be downloaded from the Internet, but these tend to be time limited (usually lasting about 30 days) so you get to try before you buy, but once the trial period is over, you're left without a back-up process again unless you're ready to pay.

- You may find any external hard disc you buy is complete with a back-up utility of its own that can save you money. Use it if you don't have anything else, as they are normally robust enough for most 'home' uses.

BACK-UP TO EXTERNAL HARD DISC

Probably the most common way to back-up your data is to use a high-capacity external hard disc. This is because with such a disc, you can set up a back-up protocol that happens automatically – so you don't have to remember to do it! And because you don't have to intervene to change discs (as with a CD or DVD back-up) it is very convenient. One drawback is that the external hard disc can crash so you may still need another strategy to back-up *its* data!

Step 2:
Click 'next' to skip the opening page and choose 'back-up files and settings' from the second page. Now click 'next' and you should see the 'What to back-up' page.

Step 3:
Choose what to back-up, but if you're tempted to click 'All information on this computer', which backs-up everything on your computer, think again - your back-up could be many gigabytes of data. Choose the location of your image files and the 'My Documents and Settings' option to get other data files (including e-mail messages and address books).

Step 4:
If you know that data is stored elsewhere (say on an external hard disc already connected to your PC) click 'Let me choose what to back-up'. Browse the 'My Computer' folder to select the files and folders you need to back-up.

Step 5:
Next, decide where to store your backed-up files. On the 'Destination' page, Windows will ask to point to a back-up location. It assumes you'll back-up everything into a single folder; choose a location for that folder and

give it a name such as 'All My Back-Ups'. It'll actually try to point to the 'A' or 'floppy drive', but you'll need hundreds of floppy discs for your images, so browse to the correct location (say a DVD burner or external hard disc – whichever you'll be using) and after you've chosen the location, click 'next' to display the wizard's final page. Then click 'finish' and the back-up will start immediately.

Back-Up to CD/DVD

You can back-up manually or with a schedule to CDs and DVDs if you wish. Of course, you'll need a CD/DVD writer and blank CDs or DVDs. The biggest difference here is that you'll need to be on hand to change CDs or DVDs if they fill up before all the data is written to them. Consider this before you start, as a CD holds only around 700MB of data and a DVD about 4.7GB. If you only have a couple of gigabytes of data to back-up, then using a writable DVD is going to be the way to go. If you have a CD/DVD re-writer and re-writable discs for it, you can reuse the same CD and DVD disc (or discs) each time, saving money.

Fully Manual Back-Ups

You can of course back-up simply by making copies of the valuable data onto another hard disc, CD, or DVD. You don't need any fancy software but do need to ensure you have all your data properly organised on your hard disc so you know where everything is. The process is simply one of dragging the data files to be backed-up to the separate disc. A good idea is to create a back-up folder and date it; that way you'll be able to keep track of what's been backed-up and when.

This Plextor DVD burner is ideal for backing-up to disc, either CDs or DVDs. It comes with its own software and is simple to use with automated or manual back-ups.

Printing

You're not restricted to viewing digital images on screen. It's easy to make 'real world' prints for framing, sharing or to put into a photo album.

It's easier than you think to make prints at home, online or when shopping on the high street. Here's some key advice on getting the best from each option.

Printing Your Photos At Home

Obviously this requires you to have your own printer. If you don't have one but want the convenience of printing at home, you'll find all the buying advice you need in the topic *Which Printer?* Let's get started with a few printer basics.

Step 1:
You'll need to install the printer's software (called a print driver) on your computer to make sure the computer can 'see' the printer. However, some computer operating systems have many printer drivers built-in, so this may be a step you can skip. Check with your computer's or printer's installation instructions.

Step 2:
File > Open the image you'll be printing in your image editing software and use the **File > Print** command to activate your printer's driver controls within the software.

The print preview (right) allows paper and print size selection; the software does all the working out for your chosen settings.

Step 3:
Pick the paper and print size you need and click the print button. A new dialogue box (above) will appear which allows the changing of printer settings if required. Pick the correct paper type (many new inkjets can automatically set the paper for you), and colour options in the drop-down menus. You can also preview your print job. Set the print resolution and hit print again – the print job will start. Always double-check that the correct paper and print resolution are selected, as these are essential to get the correct quality of print.

Printing Online

Online printing is becoming more and more popular, with dedicated photo-printing web sites springing up around the globe. Using them is fairly straightforward and inexpensive; you either email in your images or upload them via the website. You pay online with a credit or debit card and then are sent the photos in the post. Make sure you use a service that is in your country though!

Ideally you'll need a broadband Internet connection (otherwise uploads will take too long). Such sites usually have virtual photo album functionality, where you can upload images and store them online - although there may be a charge for this. Then you can email links to the images for friends and family to view.

Printing in Shops

There are many retail outlets where you can take your memory card to print out images quickly and cheaply, in the same way you used to drop off your films. Some shops have print kiosks, where you insert the memory card and follow on-screen prompts to select and print the photos yourself.

However, whether you use a kiosk or an over-the-counter service, remember one thing: if you print everything on the memory card but don't have a back-up (say a CD of the images) then you will lose all the original images forever if your card is later reformatted in your camera. So, always have a CD made *and* get prints if you don't have a computer at home. That way, you can take the CD in to the shop for more prints and you never have to worry about losing images.

Using the Right Paper

There are many types of paper (or media) available for inkjet printers, and they come in a range of sizes (A4 or A3 for example) or on rolls of paper.

Using the right paper is essential - you cannot get a photo-quality print on plain paper for example. On photo paper, the paper and ink work together to give the best possible effect and to help make the print last a long time. Here's a quick run down of what to look for and when to use it.

- Plain Media: Use plain paper only for printing letters or basic graphics and text, not for photographs.

- Photo Media: Photo paper comes in glossy and matt finishes and is the best paper to use for photo-quality output as it is designed to make the most of every droplet of ink and to boost colour.

- Transfer (or T-Shirt) Media: A speciality media for printing images that can then be transferred, to a T-shirt for example, using a hot iron.

- High Resolution Media: Ideal for graphics and text (say a display banner) where perfectly smooth edges to text and colours are essential for a good impression.

- Transparency Media: Transparent media designed for presentations using overhead projectors for example.

GET THE BEST FROM YOUR PRINTER

To ensure perfect prints (or the print output you're expecting!) check these tips.

- Make sure the paper selection in the printer set-up dialogue box matches the paper you're printing on. If you choose plain paper but load photo-quality paper, the printed result will be very poor. However, many new printers automatically detect the paper and set the printer accordingly, unless you override it in the printer set-up box.

- Inkjets can print at very-high-resolution settings that are slow to print and can use a lot of expensive ink. To save ink (and time), use the lowest print resolution that's acceptable for the job at hand. A few test prints may be needed to ascertain these settings. Make a note of them for each paper type or print job (or save the settings for reuse if your software allows) then you don't have to experiment each time.

- You can alter the print size without changing the image's dimensions (also see *Resizing*) by altering its resolution in the **Image >Size** dialogue box. 300dpi is best, but don't go below 180dpi or the print quality will be poor. The lower the output dpi, the larger the print will become, which you can check in the print preview window prior to printing.

- Some image editing software can automatically create picture packages, ideal if you want more than one copy of a photo. The program does all the resizing and other changes so you can print many images on one sheet of paper.

The image size box allows adjustment of the output resolution (the document size) without altering the pixel dimensions.

The picture package dialogue box lets you select the number of images to be printed together on a single sheet of paper. Clicking on one of the image thumbnails lets you browse to another image if you want a variety of images to be printed together.

Scanning Your Photos

Scanning provides a route for traditional film images to be brought into the digital domain, where they can be manipulated and improved just like any digital image.

You probably have hundreds of old film photos that can be given a new lease of life by scanning them to create digital images (see also *Which Scanner?*). These can then be used to create a slide show or make printed copies for all the family.

Scanner Settings

It is important to scan at a setting adequate for the intended output. In other words, if you want to make an A4 photo print you'll need to scan the original at a setting that provides enough information for a good print at that size. Getting this right saves time and memory space as it is easy to create scanned images of hundreds of megabytes if you're not careful. These will take ages to scan and there will be far more image data than you need to make the print.

To control this, the resolution and the scanned image dimensions need to be adjusted but one measurement is linked to the other: adjust the finished scan dimensions and the resolution changes and vice versa.

Here a scan will be made at 200% of its original size (or double) and to do it the resolution will also double from 300ppi to 600ppi.

The original is being scanned at 100% (the same size) and at a resolution of 300ppi. The histogram display allows you to adjust the image before scanning. Note, the final scanned file size is just 6.5MB.

A typical scanner software control-box: select tasks such as creating a scan for a print or for an email. In each case, the scanner will do the hard work automatically.

Many of today's scanners have automated features to do this for you. You click a button corresponding to the task, say making a scan for a 6x4 print, and the software will do the rest.

The more adventurous can manually control these settings along with other image adjustments such as colour, contrast and brightness. The more advanced the scanner, the more options you'll be able to control.

How to Scan

Step 1:

Install the software that comes with your scanner. This is essential because without it your PC won't know the scanner is there. If your scanner installs its software as a plug-in (check the manual) used via other editing software, use the **File > Import** command in your editing software. You select your scanner's name from the list presented and then the process is the same as follows.

GET THE BEST FROM YOUR SCANNER

300ppi is the optimal resolution to scan at for prints, and 72ppi is sufficient for on-screen display. Here's a quick guide to the (approximate) file sizes you should make for various tasks.

Scans for Inkjet Photo Printing
- Scan for A3 prints: 25MB (with compatible printers)
- Scan for A4 prints: 18MB
- Scan for 10x8 inch prints: 10MB
- Scan for 4x6 inch prints: 8MB
- Scan for 3x5 inch prints: 5MB

Scans for Email and Internet Use
- Scan for use on screen/web only: 480x320 pixels, around 0.5MB
- Scan for email to print out: 960x640 pixels, around 1MB

Step 2:

With the scanner software open, choose a task, in this case making a print, and follow the instructions depending on your choice.

In this version, you select the resolution to use and the scanner software does the rest based on the paper size chosen.

Step 3:

If you're happy with the settings, click the scan button and the scanning will commence. Many consumer-oriented scanners will have controls on the scanner itself that allow you literally to scan at the push of a button: just place the original in the scanner, press a button and it scans.

Step 4:

Once the scan's completed, **File > Save** it. If you have already selected a place for the scans to be saved, each scan will be sent to that folder.

High-end scanners have more sophisticated control options but, nonetheless, the main scanning options remain the same.

Creating Slide Shows

A great way to display your photo collection is as a slide show on-screen or even on your TV.

Creating a slide show is actually simple with easy-to-use slide show creation software. You'll need to be able to save your show to a CD or DVD in order to play it. There's a wide range of such software available. A quick search on the Internet will provide hundreds of web sites that have slide show software for sale, demo versions to try-before-you-buy or even free, shareware downloads. Most packages provide effects such as Hollywood-style transitions between each image, and even allow you to add music.

Building the Slide Show

Although Apple's iMovie and iDVD software has been used here for illustration purposes, the slide show creation process is essentially the same for most slide show packages. First, gather the images you want to put in the slide show. Once you have them organised, they must be compiled into your software's workspace either by dragging and dropping them or by clicking on 'add photo' buttons and navigating to the images.

Once the images are in place, transition effects such as fades can be added between each shot. These are normally dragged from a menu to between each shot or an 'add button' is clicked, depending on the software.

Some software will have an image quality setting control. Set it so that you have a fair balance between the quality of the image and the file size of the show. This is particularly important if you're creating a slide show on CD, where space is limited to around 700MB, rather than DVD, which can take over 4.7GB of data. The higher the quality of the images in a show, the more space they will take up on the disc.

While software differs, the process is essentially the same. Left, images for inclusion in the slide show are displayed at the right side of the screen and are dragged into the 'show' across the bottom where you can adjust their run length and running order.

In this software, the right hand side of the screen shows all of the effects, transitions, images and music which can be added to the slide show. Select as you see fit by clicking the relevant buttons. In this case, a starburst effect is shown.

Once you're happy with the sequence of images, you can follow your software instructions to add introductory text and music to the show.

In this image, music is grabbed from the list to the right and added to the slide show work area across the bottom of the screen. You can set slide shows to run for the duration of any added music too, so the images and sound will be synchronised.

Saving the Show to Disc

Once you've assembled all the parts of the slide show, you're ready to save or 'burn' the show to disc. You'll need a CD or DVD burner, either built-in to your PC or as an external device, to do this.

Some slide show programs allow you to burn directly from the software in which you built the show. Follow the on-screen guide (or wizard) once you hit the burn button or similar control, such as an 'export to disc' command. It will send your assembled slide show data to the burner.

Alternatively, the show may need to be exported to a separate CD/DVD burning program to be burnt to disc. Such programs may allow you to add chapter markers or menu screens.

Here the slide show (in this case using Apple's iDVD) has had a menu screen added in the program. Clicking the burn button starts the burn process.

Adding the Photo Files

Some slide show programs allow you to add the actual, original image files to the disc in addition to the slide show versions of the image. This is a great way of giving family members their own copy of the images, useful if they wish to make some prints for example. You must have room on the disc to be able to do this however, so if you have a large show, it's unlikely that it will all fit on a CD. Use a DVD instead.

Emailing Photos

Email is one of the fastest ways to get your latest shots to friends and family. Here are a few tips to make it even better for you and them.

To get your photos ready for emailing to friends and family, the most important consideration is the image's file size. Not everyone has broadband Internet access so sending large files by email may just jam up their system and make it expensive for them to download the pictures.

As some recipients may want to print the photos, while others just like to look at the images on screen, you can adapt the image sizes you send accordingly.

Resize the Images

As we've already seen in the *Resizing* topic earlier in the book, it's a straightforward process to resize the images ready for email. Let's begin by looking at the 'start' size for an image you might want to share via email.

Checking Image Size

To check the picture's dimensions, open the image and use the **Image > Resize Image** command. In this case, the shot to be emailed is a 15MB file at 300ppi with 23x15 cm dimensions. This is far too large to email.

Emailing for Screen Viewing

To resize this image to both a reasonable size in terms of viewing the image, and also a file size small enough for emailing, first check the 'resize' button in the resize image dialogue box. Change the 300ppi setting to 72ppi, the default resolution for computer screen viewing. Now the file size has plummeted to only 882KB and the pixel dimensions have dropped to 672x448 pixels. However, the document size is untouched.

Finally, **File > Save As** the image using a JPEG compression level of about 5 in the dialogue box that appears. This will provide a small email file without harsh compression, preserving image quality.

Emailing for Printing

With the same image as an example, we go through the exact same process but this time, instead of changing the ppi figure, we adjust the pixel dimensions. An image set to around 800 pixels on its longest edge (and left at 300ppi) will provide an image that has enough data for a decent 6x4 inch photo print and yet it will produce a file small enough to email.

The 1.22Mb file this has created must be saved using the **File >Save As** routine again, but this time you can adjust the JPEG compression in order to suit the Internet connection speed at the recipient's end. If they're using a dial-up modem, use a JPEG setting of around 2, but if they have broadband then a setting of 7 should suffice. Of course, you can successfully email the unaltered image if required with broadband connections, assuming it's not hundreds of megabytes in size!

Sending the Email

Once the image has been resized successfully, you can send the email using your standard email software. Compose and write the email in your normal way and then drag and drop the image (or images) into the message as an attachment. Or you can click on the add button to browse the computer's hard disc to find the photos you require. Click choose to select the pictures, which then appear in your newly composed email as attachments. Your email can now be sent as usual.

Microsoft's Entourage email program has been used here to show how the images being emailed are held within the email as attachments. You can either drag and drop them into the attachment window or click add to browse the photos and then click choose to attach them.

Creating A Photo Website

Putting your images on the Internet is an ideal way to showcase your pictures or create a themed website. And it can be much less technical than you might think.

You don't have to let your images languish on your computer's hard disc, you can share them on the Internet. It's easy enough to set up your own web site, perhaps to promote a club or hobby, or even just for your family snaps.

You won't have to learn any special programming languages, as most image editing software comes with an automated web gallery building function. It allows you to build a web site of your own images easily and quickly, where all the complicated programming code (HTML) used to make web sites work is written for you.

Constructing a Web Gallery

If you want to build an online photo gallery or create a web-based portfolio of your images, modern image editing software can achieve this relatively quickly. While the different software packages vary to a degree, the process described below is much the same. Here we use screen shots from Adobe's Photoshop Elements 3 as a guide.

Step 1:

First we must set up the images correctly by putting the images you want online together into a folder on your hard disc. Call this the 'source folder'. Create another folder called the 'destination folder'. When you've finished, this folder will contain all the web image files and the HTML for the web gallery.

Step 2:

Using your software, you'll need to start the web gallery build. Use **File > Create Web Photo Gallery** (or your software's version of this) and use the styles menu to choose a gallery design. Preview and select the one you like the best.

In this screen shot the gallery's style, name and other information are all entered. The style is previewed in the small window to the right.

Step 3:

Select the previously created 'source' and 'destination' folders for your web site. Source images will be processed and altered and then copies of them placed into the destination folder. Also, pick a size for the images to be changed to, for online viewing (in this case 450 pixels) with a JPEG quality setting of 5 in this software's options menu.

The source and destination folders have been selected as have the image dimensions and JPEG quality. Now the images will be resized and optimised properly for your website.

Pick simple colours and plain backgrounds to make the most of the images on your website.

Step 4:

As with Step 3 above, you'll need to decide on the size of the thumbnail images for your gallery. Here we've picked 75 pixels with a border of 2 pixels to help define them on screen. Some software will allow you to customise the thumbnail size to a large extent, but as with all things 'web', the larger the images the more memory they'll take and the slower the web site may be to use once it's up and running online.

You can change the thumbnail image size and border as you wish or, depending on the software, use the drop-down 'size' menu which will choose for you.

Step 5:

Now pick the various custom colours for your web site, such as the link colours, colour of text and the background. Avoid patterned backgrounds – keep it simple – otherwise, the gallery can cause eyestrain if it's too 'busy'. Black is an ideal background for images as it helps show them to their best advantage. However, any neutral colour is also gentle on the eye: the template used in our example is grey.

Step 6:

You might want to consider including some form of copyright or security information. That way, visitors to the gallery cannot download your photos and use them without your permission (see the *Copyright* topic for more on this). Here, custom text has been included from the options menu. This is embedded into the online images and adds to the security.

Once you're happy click OK and the software starts compiling the site.

You can add copyright and security information into your images if required, for example if you want to sell your photos.

Step 7:

When the site has been built, use a web browser (such as Internet Explorer) and **File > Open** the '**index.html**' file created in the destination folder. This will now contain all your web gallery data. Incidentally, never move files from this folder or the gallery will stop working. Your web gallery should appear in the web browser window. This last step is just to check that your site looks as you intended and that all the links work.

GETTING THE GALLERY ONLINE

Once you have your web site built, all that's left to do is move the web site onto the Internet. You can upload the destination folder of the newly created web gallery to your web host or Internet Service Provider, which will then make the site 'live'. However, check with your provider for the exact process as it can vary depending on their site set-up.

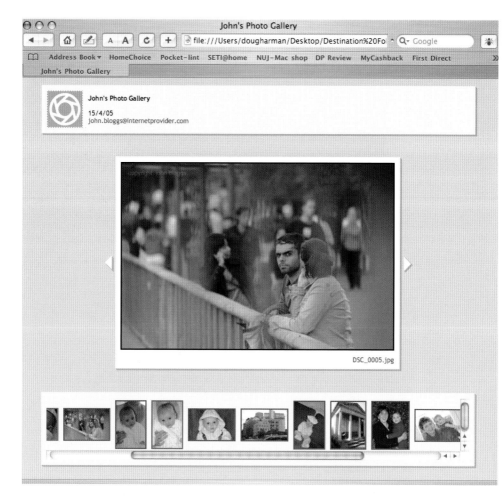

The finished web gallery, with thumbnails across the bottom in this example and large images displayed with left and right arrows for extra navigation. You can click a thumbnail to open the images too.

Making A Portfolio

If you're serious about your photography, particularly if you want to sell your images, you'll need to compile a professional portfolio of work.

Creating a portfolio of images is not just a matter of getting all your images together and printing them or putting them on a website. If you intend to make any money, you'll need to cherry-pick the very best of your images and use only those. Being critical is essential as competition is fierce, and unless you focus on your best shots, you're unlikely to succeed.

An Internet or on-disc portfolio is a must, but you also need to have a high-quality print portfolio.

Print Portfolio

You'll need to get your very best images printed using high-quality photo output and ideally at a large enough size to give the viewer a good impression of what can be achieved with them. Print no smaller than A4 on fade resistant photo paper and buy a good quality portfolio folder with sleeves to house the prints. Beware, less expensive portfolios often use plastic pages that seep chemicals and can damage your prints over time.

If you have stunning images that you might want to sell or hope to make money from, a portfolio - online and as prints - will be required.

Online and On-Disc Portfolios

You'll need to put your portfolio on the Internet (see *Creating a Photo Website*) or on disc (see *Creating Slide Shows*). Ensure each image is annotated with its technical details, and that the slide show is made at the highest quality possible. Sacrifice the number of images in a show to ensure high quality. It's better to have numerous discs than all the images crammed as low-resolution files onto just one.

Organise all the images by content type: architecture, landscapes, portraits, animals etc. This makes relevant images easier to find and if you don't have software able to do this, consider getting the portfolio made professionally. Scrimping here could cost you money in the end.

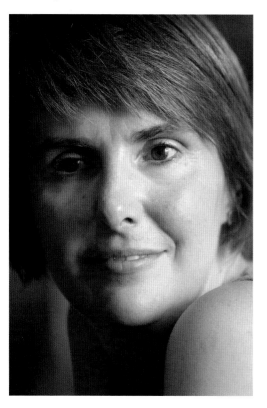

INCLUDING IMAGE INFORMATION

There are key details that should always be associated with your images in any portfolio. Some may seem unnecessary, but all are, in fact, vital. Magazine editors, for instance, are likely to require detailed text information for captions and if it is with the image already it saves them time, making them more likely to use your image over someone else's.

- **Copyright information**: Include your name and contact details with each image. On prints NEVER write on the back of the print itself. Use special stickers or frame the shots in card borders (from art shops) and include the details on that. Digital images have the detail automatically appended with each image and it can then be viewed as the image is displayed.

- **Image technical data**: The shutter speed, focal length, sensitivity setting and lens aperture should all be included. All this information is to be found within the image EXIF data, using your image editing software.

- **Date and location**: Include the date the image was made and the location where it was taken/what's in the shot.

- **Image dimensions**: Include the image's pixel dimensions and file size.

Portraits such as this can be an ideal way to start building a portfolio from your images. Practise on family and friends to help hone your skills and get the perfect photo for the portfolio you're building.

Making Money

Making money from your photography is more achievable than you might think.

Gaining income from your photographs doesn't always mean you'll need professional camera gear and the expense that goes with it because, today, the fastest route to getting your images to market is via the Internet.

But if you want to make money from your photos, family snaps won't be the type of image people want to buy, and you'll need to shoot images that are less personal and more commercial. It's best to have a commercial target market in mind, and then shoot images that are relevant to it.

If, for instance, you want to get your images into magazines, competitions are good ways to start as this helps to discover what's acceptable. The classic tropical beach with palm trees you see in holiday brochures would be an ideal example of an ever-popular shot. Landscapes and architecture are always in demand, particularly if you get a novel angle on the subject. Macro style images of flowers and plants are good too. But what are the routes to making money that you can consider?

Images such as this shot of Egyptian hieroglyphics are classic shots which can be used time and again, from historical publications to holiday brochures.

Put Your Photos Online

We've already looked at building a web site from your images, but if you're going to take this seriously, you'll need to use only the very best of your photos. Eventually you'll need to think about getting a professionally built site, as competition is very stiff. This will cost money but will give you more chance of reaching a wider audience.

Set Up An Exhibition

Setting up an exhibition of your work will raise your profile, but this can be expensive and time-consuming. Look to local businesses such as cafes, to see if they would consider hanging framed prints for you (there may be a small commission) with your details on each photo.

Join The Professionals

Join a professional photo society or your local camera club. These will be able to offer advice on selling and improving your photography and have many connections that will help you get your images out to a wider audience.

Print Postcards Or Calendars

Having postcards or calendars of your images printed is another good way to circulate your photos more widely. However, depending on how many you have printed, the cost can be prohibitive and you'll need to plan in advance who to send them to or where to display them. You could even start selling them at local markets.

Join An Image Library

Image libraries are businesses that hold photos for many different photographers and act as an agency, selling the use of your images to magazines for example. You get a fee each time an image is used and the library takes a percentage of that money. Most libraries have web sites too. Many image libraries have very specific criteria for the images they want (digital or otherwise and particularly for file size limits) so you'll need to contact them in advance to make sure your images are of the required type/standard.

'Timeless' images such as flowers as in this example are another great image type to use if you want to make money from your photography. And make sure you always shoot images at the highest possible quality to ensure you can reproduce the images at a variety of sizes, particularly larger prints which can also be framed to hang on a wall.

Copyright

You'll need to be aware of copyright issues in our digital age, particularly if you want to sell your photographs.

Copyright is the term describing the law that protects you from the use or abuse of your images by others without your permission. For example, if one of your photos was required for use in a magazine article, the copyright for that image rests with you, the photographer, and the magazine could not use it without a payment to you or your permission to do so.

Anyone who copies or reproduces an image without first paying – or at least getting permission from – the author to do so, is said to be breaching the author's copyright. While legal specifics vary from country to country (it's best to check) and can be dependent upon what is negotiated at the time, this is the basic rule.

This image has the author's name embedded for copyright information, preventing this image being used without payment. This is an ideal tactic for portfolio images off- or online. To obtain the image for reproduction, the author needs to be contacted and the non-marked image then supplied for use.

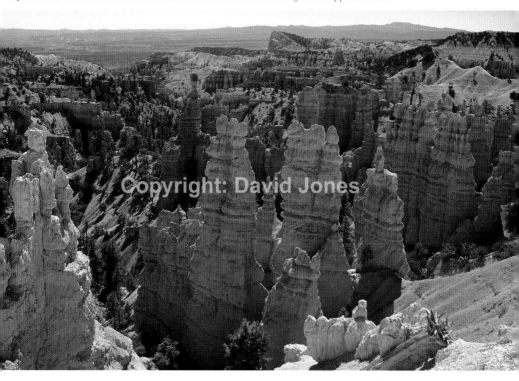

Copyright: David Jones

Types Of Copyright

Some companies might want to buy the entire copyright (called 'all rights') for any image, and this means that from that point on they don't need to pay you again. They have effectively bought the copyright from you and it is theirs to do with as they see fit. You should place a higher price on images you sell in this way. Typically, however, most photographers sell 'single-use rights' in their images, which means the photographer retains the copyright and can re-use and re-sell the image repeatedly.

How To Get Copyrighted

Copyright arises automatically in all works of art, including photography, writing and digital images as they're created. No formal registration is required to receive the basic legal protection this affords in over 140 countries around the world.

Protecting Your Images

- The Internet: While you cannot stop people from downloading your images, you can take precautions to stop them using them elsewhere without payment. Use watermarking technology (it will cost money but embeds a hidden code in the photo which is unique to you and which can be retrieved later using special software) or add your name to the image (as shown, left). This can be done discreetly in a corner of the shot; it's an ideal tactic for portfolios too.

- Ensure any images you put on the Internet are large enough to be viewed at a good size on screen, but small enough in terms of file size to make them useless for printing.

- In Print: Watermarking works well on prints too, but you are unable to either reduce the file size or add your name to the print as you can on digital images. You can, however, put a sticker on the reverse of the image with your copyright details. Remember, copying a print (a scan for example) without payment to you, or your permission, will breach your copyright.

Royalty-Free Images

These images are photos in which the copyright has been bought outright and which are then assembled, say on a CD, for which there's a charge. These shots can then be used (even commercially in many instances) without incurring another fee from the author for their use. The one-off charge for a royalty-free CD in this example is all that needs to be paid.

If you don't want to 'ruin' an illustrative shot with a big copyright notice, you can also create smaller, less obtrusive text and place it out of the way in a corner of the image as shown here.

Glossary

Aberration Imperfections in an image caused by deficiencies within a lens or optical system. These can be aberrations of shape, sharpness and colour.

Ambient Light The natural light in a scene.

Aperture The circular opening inside a camera's lens that can change in diameter to control the amount of light reaching the camera's sensor. Apertures are expressed in F-stops; the lower the number, the larger the aperture. For instance, an aperture of F2.8 is larger than one of F8. Aperture and shutter speed together control the total amount of light reaching the sensor. Large apertures pass more light through to the sensor. Many cameras will have an aperture priority mode allowing adjustment of the aperture to your own liking. (See also Shutter Speed)

Application A computer program, such as an image editing package or a web browser such as Internet Explorer.

Archival Quality Term used to denote materials having a high degree of permanence. If the longevity of a material (such as printing papers and CDs or DVDs) is said to exceed an acceptable defined time period before starting to degrade, it is said to be of archival quality.

Artefact An unwanted visual aberration within a digital

image, often caused by over-compression.

Aspect Ratio The proportions (or ratio) of a picture's width to its height.

Backing-Up Making copies of important computer files and applications/programs in case the originals are damaged and cannot be accessed.

Bit The basic unit of information used in computing. A bit represents a one or a zero, a true or a false or 'on' or 'off' in a computer.

Buffer A memory reservoir built into digital cameras that stores the photos before they are written to the memory card.

Burning (CD/DVD) Creating a copy of your images by electronically saving image files onto an optical disc such as a DVD or CD. (See also Writing)

Burning (image editing) Selectively darkening part of a photo with an image editing program.

Byte A data 'chunk' made up of eight bits.

Cast The effect of one (unwanted) colour dominating the look of an image. Often caused by exposure errors or incorrect settings of a digital camera's white balance for the ambient/artificial lighting.

CCD Charge coupled device.

One of the two main types of image sensors (see also CMOS) used in digital cameras. When you take a picture, the CCD is struck by light coming through the lens and the millions of tiny pixels that make up the CCD convert this light into electrons. The number of electrons is measured and converted to a digital value, a step that occurs outside the CCD, in the camera's analogue-to-digital converter.

CD-R CD-Recordable. A compact disc that holds around 650 to 700MB of digital information. A CD-R disc can only be written to once but is an ideal storage medium for your digital photos.

CD-ROM Compact disc read-only-memory. A type of CD similar to a normal audio CD but optimised for data storage.

CD-RW CD-Rewritable. Similar to a CD-R, except a CD-RW can be written and erased many times. Suited to many back-up tasks, but not for long-term storage.

CMOS Complementary metal-oxide semiconductor. One of the two main types of image sensors (see CCD above) used in digital cameras. Its basic function is the same as that of a CCD.

CMYK Cyan, Magenta, Yellow, Black. The four colours (or ink sets) of many photo-quality printers. Some more expensive photo-printers use six, seven or even eight inks to achieve smoother, more photographic prints.

CompactFlash (TYPE I or II) A common type of digital camera memory card. There are two types of cards, Type I and Type II, that vary in their thickness, Type I being the thinner.

Compression Reducing the file size of digital data files by removing redundant and/or non-critical information within a digital image, helping to maximise storage space.

Contrast The difference between the darkest and lightest areas in a photograph. The greater the difference, the higher the contrast.

Copyright Legal protection against copying and the specific rights allowing copying applying to original works such as photographs. Copyright arises automatically whenever an original work, such as a photo, is created.

Depth of Field (DOF) The distance between the nearest and farthest points that appear in acceptably sharp focus in a photo. DOF varies with lens aperture, focal length and camera-to-subject distance.

Digital Camera A camera that captures a photographic image using an electronic imaging sensor (see CCD or CMOS) instead of traditional film.

Dodging Selectively lightening part of a photo, using image editing software.

DOF see Depth of Field

Downloading Moving computer data from one location to another. Often used to describe the transfer of data from the Internet. Also used to describe the transfer of photos from a camera memory card to a computer.

dpi Dots per inch. Measurement of the resolution of a digital photo print or digital device such as an inkjet printer. The higher the dpi number, the greater the resolution. (Also see ppi)

D-SLR Digital, single-lens reflex camera. A digital camera that allows the scene to be viewed through the lens that will take the photo.

DVD Digital versatile disc. A type of high-capacity optical recording media available in DVD-R and DVD-RW types (similar to CDs) but able to store 4.7gigabytes of data.

EXIF Exchangeable image file. Image data (such as shutter speed, aperture and ISO) that's stored directly in the image file generated by a digital camera. The data can be read by any application that supports JPEG and TIFF file formats, such as web browsers and image editing applications.

Exposure The total amount of light allowed to fall on a digital camera's sensor during the process of taking a photograph. Exposure is measured in EV and the higher the EV, the more light there is.

External Flash An accessory flash unit (or flashgun) that is triggered by the camera or the light from the camera's internal flash.

File A computer document such as an image file.

Fill Flash A flash technique common to most digital cameras used to brighten deep shadow areas, for example, outdoors on sunny days. This mode forces the flash to fire even in bright light.

Filter (photography) A camera accessory made from (usually) optical glass, which is inserted into the optical path to provide a specific effect, such as adding an artificial colour. It can be a square filter mounted in a holder or (more commonly) a disc, which can be screwed in front of the lens.

Filter (software) A software tool that can be used to produce special effects.

Fire An often-used slang term for taking a picture; as in 'fire the shutter'.

FireWire (also known as IEEE 1394) A cabling technology used to transfer data to and from digital devices at high speed. Many professional digital cameras and memory card readers connect to the computer over FireWire.

Focal Length The distance between the sensor (or film for traditional cameras) and the optical centre of a lens when that lens is focused on infinity. Focal length is marked in millimetres on the lens (or mount) on those cameras with adjustable focal lengths such as a zoom compact camera.

Formatting The act of writing a file system onto a computer disc or memory card that completely deletes all the previous information and file structure on that disc or card, replacing it with a fresh structure ready for new information. Formatting is the recommended method of clearing a camera's memory card.

F-stop (or F-number) The measure of the size of a camera lens's aperture. The higher the F-stop, the smaller the aperture and vice versa.

Gamut The total range of colours reproduced by a device such as a digital camera, scanner or printer.

Gif Graphical interchange format file. A bitmap graphical format, ideal for logos, line drawings or images with solid colours.

Gigabyte (GB) A gigabyte is the mount of memory equal to 1024 megabytes (or 1,073,741,824 bytes) of information.

Greyscale An image made of varying tones of black and white.

Highlights The brightest parts of a photo.

Histogram A graphic representation of the range of tones from dark to light in a photo. Many digital cameras include a histogram feature facilitating a precise check on the exposure of the photo.

Image Editor A computer program used to alter the appearance of a photo.

Image Resolution The total number of pixels used to make up a digital photo.

Inkjet A type of printer that fires ink droplets onto paper through tiny nozzles.

ISO Sensitivity Digital cameras use the same rating system as for film to denote the camera sensor's sensitivity to light. Often a control for adjusting the ISO speed is included; some cameras adjust it automatically depending on the lighting conditions. The higher the ISO number (100, 200, 400 etc.) the more sensitive to light the camera becomes, but as ISO speed climbs, image quality drops.(See also Noise)

JPEG A standard for compressing image data. A JPEG is not, strictly speaking, a file format, it is a compression method used within a file format (see EXIF). Referred to as a 'lossy' format, some image quality is 'lost' in achieving the JPEG compression.

Kilobyte (KB) A unit of measurement equal to 1000 bytes.

LCD Liquid crystal display. A type of colour screen often used on the rear of a digital camera to help with composition and to display the photo once it's taken, and to display setting/control menus.

Media Generic term used for any material that information can be written to and stored on. Digital photography storage media can include memory cards, CDs and DVDs while in printing the paper used is often described as print media.

Megabyte (MB) A measurement of data storage equal to 1024 kilobytes (KB).

Megapixel Equal to one million

pixels (or 1MP). The higher the number of megapixels, the higher the resolution of a digital camera is said to be.

Memory Stick A flash-based storage device for photos.

MultiMedia Card A type of flash-based memory card similar to Secure Digital and able to support multiple data types (audio, image or digital movie data for example).

NiMH Nickel metal-hydride. A type of rechargeable battery, ideal for running digital cameras and flashes.

Noise (in an image) Unwanted random artefacts within an image created by the electronics within a camera and other environmental factors such as heat. Often used together with the term signal-to-noise ratio, which describes the ratio between actual image information (the signal) and the level of background noise. Many digital cameras have internal processing to keep noise to a minimum: a high signal-to-noise ratio is desirable.

Operating System (OS) The base software needed to manage a computer/device's hardware and software applications; examples include Windows and Mac OS.

Panning Photo technique in which the camera follows a moving subject, keeping the subject sharp whilst blurring the background giving a sense of motion to the photo.

PDF Portable document format. A document file that can be looked at anywhere if you have Adobe Acrobat Reader software.

PICT A file format used primarily for on-screen images.

Pixel A picture element. Digital photographs are composed of millions of them; they are the building blocks of a digital photo and consist of a small light-sensitive photo site, a micro lens and the necessary wiring.

Pixelated Referring to images of poor quality where the balance between image resolution and output is not correct when printing. For example, if a low-resolution image (say 72dpi) is enlarged by 200% and printed, the pixels become visible – hence pixelated – giving a jagged effect to the printed image.

Plug-In Software programs that enhance other computer programs and applications. There are plug-ins for Internet browsers, graphics programs and image editing applications.

ppi Pixels per inch. Measurement of the resolution of a digital image (or of a scan made by a scanner) is made in ppi. The higher the ppi number, the greater the resolution. (See also dpi)

RAM Random access memory. The type of computer storage whose contents can be accessed in any order, used by your applications for processing and temporary storage. (See also ROM)

RAW Image format where the data is unprocessed (by the camera) as it comes directly off the CCD. Mostly used by professional photographers who want to get specific effects from their images. Often provides superior quality (in an image editor) to a camera's internal image processing.

Redeye The reflected red glow from a subject's eyes when light from a flash is coloured by the blood vessels in the retina. Most common when light levels are low indoors, with babies or outdoors at night.

Resolution (of a lens, or resolving power) The ability of a lens or optical system to show fine detail. The higher the resolving power of a lens the more detail can be captured.

RGB Red, green and blue. The three primary colours into which digital cameras split/convert an image.

ROM Read-only memory. Computer memory whose contents can be accessed and read but cannot be changed. (See also RAM)

Saturation Measure of how richly colours are rendered in a photo.

Secure Digital A type of flash-memory storage card with built-in copyright security facilities.

Sensitivity see ISO

Sensor see CCD; CMOS

Sharpness The perceived clarity of detail within a photo. Can usually be adjusted in the camera or later using an image editing package.

Shutter Speed Measure of how long the shutter stays open as the photo is taken. The slower the shutter speed, the longer the exposure is said to be. For example, a shutter speed set to 1/250 means the shutter will be open for exactly 1/250th of one second. Shutter speed and aperture together control the amount of light reaching the sensor. Many digital cameras have a shutter priority mode allowing you to set the shutter speed to your liking. (See also Aperture)

Signal-to-noise ratio see Noise

SmartMedia A wafer-thin flash-based memory card.

Thumbnail A small version of a photo. Image browsers commonly display many thumbnails at a time.

TIFF Tagged image file format. A widely used file format for storing greyscale and colour images.

USB Universal serial bus. A protocol for transferring data to and from digital devices. Many digital cameras and memory card readers connect to the USB port on a computer.

White Balance A function on the camera that allows compensation for the different colours of light being emitted by different light sources. (See also Cast)

WiFi A method of connecting cameras, printers and PCs without using any cables.

Writing (a file) The process of outputting a data file to a CD using a device that 'burns' the data to the disc.

xD Picture Card A tiny flash-based storage card typically used in Olympus and Fujifilm digital cameras.

Index

Photography Credits

The publishers are grateful to the following for permission to use their photographs:

All photographs **David Jones** except:

Doug Harman pages 39, 65, 70, 73, 74, 75 (right), 105, 106, 107, 114, 141, 142, 143, 151, 176, 177, 198, 200, 201, 206, 212

Special thanks to all the manufacturers who granted permission to use their product shots:

Apacer, Apple, ArcSoft, Canon, CCS, Elio, Epson, Fujifilm, HP, Intro 2020, JASC, Konica, Minolta, Lexar, Maxtor, Nikon, Nixvue, Olympus, Panasonic, Pentax, Plextor, Ricoh, SanDisk, Sigma, Slik, Sony, Velbon, Wacom

The publishers would like to extend particular thanks to Adobe for permission to use the image on the front jacket, on page 113 and all Photoshop screen shots.

The Author

Doug Harman has over 15 years' experience as a journalist, writer, photographer, and digital camera and technology tester. He has written extensively for a multitude of digital photography magazines and websites, including *Amateur Photographer*, *What Digital Camera*, *Total Digital Photography*, *Professional Photographer* and *Photography Monthly*. He is also the cofounder of *US3 Media Ltd*.

The Photographer

David Jones is a professional photographer with an extensive commercial portfolio, particularly in the fashion and advertising industries. He has also been widely exhibited and contributed photographs to many magazines and books, including *Brunel*, *How to Keep Dinosaurs* and *Master Chef*.